HONEY, I'M HOME

How to Prevent or Resolve Marriage Conflicts

Caused by Retirement

Robert P. Delamontagne Ph.D.

A Retiring Mind® Book

Honey, I'm Home: How to Prevent or Resolve Marital Conflicts Caused by Retirement

ISBN 978-0-615-43513-8

For Marie,
Whose Light Still Shines

Contents

Prologue

JOHN HENRY

John Henry worked for the railroad for 35 years as a Chief Engineer. Every day he walked to the train station, got on the train and rode it until the end of the day. He was very successful because he could keep his employees and passengers happy and the train running on time. Over the years he became admired by all and was considered one of the very best managers in the entire company. He won award after award for the performance of his train.

One day John Henry turned 65 and he realized that it was his retirement day. He walked to the train station as usual, got onto the train and talked to the same people as always, only this day was different. He realized he would never ride on this train again. Everyone knew this was his last day and they had a big celebration of his retirement. John Henry went along with all the fuss, but felt a sense of sadness he cleverly disguised – it felt like a bittersweet occasion to him.

At the end of the day he got off the train and stepped onto the platform. He acknowledged all the people he saw waving out of the train car windows – familiar faces he would miss. As the train left the station he stood there watching it disappear down the tracks. He heard the train whistle far off in the distance. He turned and started for home.

As he walked he felt a sense of relief that he would not have the responsibility for budgets, schedules and employees ever again, but also a deep sense of loss because he liked managing the train and the challenge of meeting its schedule. As he neared home he wondered about the future now that he would be free of his daily obligations – what would it be like to spend most of his time at home with his wife?

He entered the front door and hollered, "Honey, I'm Home." Under his breath he whispered *forever*.

✳✳✳

She decided to make a special dinner for her husband to celebrate his retirement. She arranged the flowers, prepared his favorite meal, opened a bottle of wine, set the table and lit the candles. She then turned on some background music to set the mood and casually glanced at her appointment calendar. She saw a busy week ahead.

First there was the book club meeting this evening; it was her turn to lead the discussion. Tomorrow was her tennis luncheon. The next day she worked at the library all day. Sarah, their daughter, had called and asked her to baby-sit later in the week – just the usual hectic routine.

She heard the front door open and her husband announce, "Honey, I'm Home," and under her breath she whispered, *forever.* She wondered what he was going to do with himself while she was gone.

Preface

Retirement is like flying an airplane blindfolded. You don't know where you are and you can't see what's ahead of you. It is not until you actually hit something that you know you are in trouble, and by then it's too late to prevent it. Who would ever expect that retirement could cause serious marital conflicts? Not me. Why then did I begin hearing things from my wife like, "Stop trying to organize my day?" "I'm sorry I cannot do that with you today, I have made other plans (that didn't include me)." "Stop directing me. I am not one of your employees!" Here's my favorite: "Why don't you go find something to do (that didn't include her)." After 40 years of marriage and my recent retirement, I realized I had entered a new stage of connubial bliss—and I wasn't sure I liked it.

In all honesty, I have a great marriage and my wife and I are very compatible souls. We seldom argue and can usually work things out without a great deal of stress. Of course, we have had our moments like all marriages, but on the whole I couldn't ask for a better partner. So if I was hitting some marital headwinds after my retirement, what was going on in those marriages that were a bit more contentious, with considerably less compatibility? I didn't think much more about it until a chance encounter brought it back to my attention.

It occurred in a meeting I had with a lovely loan officer who worked for a financial institution where I was applying for a loan. During our meeting she asked me how I was spending my time after retirement. I mentioned I had recently written a book on how to make the psychological adjustment to retirement. She immediately expressed a desire to learn more about the book. As I began to share the results of my research she intimated she was currently experiencing severe conflicts with her husband caused by his recent retirement. It was to the point that they had entered marriage counseling to resolve their differences. It was easy to see this was a painful topic and I appreciated her trust in sharing her story with me.

After I left the meeting I wondered how widespread this problem could be. It seemed logical that marital discord could be a product of this challenging transition to a new stage of life. I then began speaking with friends and acquaintances who had recently retired and raised the question of whether or not retirement had placed any additional stress or strain on their marriages. In almost every instance the answer was a definitive yes. This is supported by The Office of National Statistics data showing that the rate of divorce is dropping sharply in every age group, except those over 60[1].

My interest in writing this book is based on my personal belief that marriage is sacred. It is the most important relationship that most of us will have in our lifetime. For much of the world, it is viewed as a spiritual commitment made to God, which is accompanied by formal blessings from a church or other religious institution. The following comments overheard at a wedding in France clearly express this perception of marriage:

> Marriage is not something people figure out for themselves...or invent. People – men and women – do not create themselves. Nor do they create the kind of unique and inexplicable union that takes place between them. It is something that was not designed by us. And it is not something that we can improve upon. Marriage is a divine thing, not a man-made thing.2

---

[1] An Inconvenient Truth About Late-Life Divorce, Times Online, June 4, 2010

[2] The Daily Reckoning, 8/9/2010

I realize there can be no greater source of pleasure than a marriage based on love, trust and commitment. On the other hand, there can be no greater source of pain than a marriage rife with anger, discord and disappointment. If you fall into the latter category at the present time, rest assured that help is on the way. I am confident this book can help you through the perplexing and often painful emotions that you may be experiencing and I want you to know that a new level of love and peace is possible for you. For those who are just preparing for retirement, this book will help you to identify potential problem areas that could be lurking in the shadows and provide the guidance you need to address these issues before they erupt into conflicts of a serious nature.

As we move through this book I will be leading you through progressive stages of knowledge and understanding. It is my wish and expectation that you will gain some new insights along the way to help you to attain a higher level of satisfaction with your marriage.

This book covers the following topics:

- Primary causes of marital conflict in retirement.
- The role the heart plays in love relationships.
- An analysis of your personality type.

- Identification of your spouse's personality type.

- Exploration of potential areas of conflict caused by personality type differences between spouses.

- Recommendations to improve the overall quality of your relationship.

- A process for sharing heartfelt feelings with your spouse.

- Guidelines for implementing life changes that will reduce the stress in your marriage and accelerate your personal growth.

Of course, you know words on a page don't carry much power to change behavior and resolve interpersonal issues. Words are symbols twice removed from reality. Change comes from the experience of applying new insights and understanding to your relationship in everyday life. The intent of this book is to provide the self-awareness and guidance you need to increase the overall quality of the bond you share with your spouse. Both partners should read it simultaneously, chapter by chapter. Think of it as a relationship workbook that requires active participation rather than just passive reading. It introduces concepts and experiences that serve as invitations for change and greater understanding.

You will encounter the image shown below at strategic points throughout the book.

It is a recommendation that you and your partner stop and share your thoughts, feelings and insights before moving on. Although this book is focused on those planning for, or in, retirement, it also offers the opportunity for those in earlier stages of life to benefit from the contents of these pages.

I realize there is often a great deal of anxiety associated with the work required to improve love relationships. There is no analytical process or easy solution to be employed because it is all about deep feelings and, at times, raw emotions. After 43 years of marriage I also realize any relationship, no matter how good it may be, can stand a tune-up every now and again because we are constantly being transformed by life events. Retirement introduces us to a new set of challenges and forces us to address personal issues that may have lain dormant for years. As Joseph

Chilton Pearce states, "Relationship is all there is and what the heart longs for."[3]

Now, with time pressing on - change is coming.

---

[3] Joseph Chilton Pearce, The Death of Religion and the Rebirth of Spirit, Rochester, Vermont, Park Street Press, 2007, Pg. 123.

Chapter 1

The Causes of Marital Conflict in Retirement

I said for better or worse...but I never said for lunch.
— Night Fall, Nelson DeMille

Marriage between two people is so complex that it is almost impossible to completely understand the broad array of human variables entwined within the relationship. For example, a few major areas in which partners differ are early family influences, psychological health, and most importantly, personality type. Let's not forget the multifaceted differences that exist between the sexes. These distinguishing features are dynamic in nature and serve as major influences throughout our lives. They differentiate us as individuals and naturally serve, together, as the signature for our identities. As we go through life they represent a commingled expression of all that we are as human beings. They function as vertexes of our identities; however, they also represent areas of potential conflict within our marriages. In fact, if each of us could identify and chart our own unique life configuration and then compare and contrast it with that of our partner prior to our nuptials, no one would ever get married. Most of us would run for the hills because we would see no way to overcome the large disparities caused by diverging interests, aptitudes, ambitions and personal histories. Fortunately none of us enter marriage with such an elaborate comparison because, at the time, we are operating under the intoxicating influence of the heart.

Of course, there are structural causes of marital conflict, such as financial crisis, health problems or family strife. These types of problems can place great stress on a marriage because they may appear insurmountable, at least in the short term, and may require life-changing adaptation that can be very painful. Since these causes do not have to do with personal differences, we are going to omit them from our discussion.

Retirement

When I retired at the age of 63 I thought I was well prepared for this new stage of life. I sold the company I had founded and managed for 25 years, and at long last achieved financial security. But it came as a shock to me when I discovered I was not really prepared for my retirement on an emotional level. It should not have come as a surprise, considering I lived my life in a very intense and structured way for 35 years, and then one day all that familiar structure and mental stimulation were gone. As a result I began experiencing intense irritability and emotional stress. I also noticed more annoyance and frustration in the relationship with my wife. Over time the situation did not improve and I decided I needed to take action as quickly as possible.

Why didn't anyone warn me that retirement often demands a major psychological adjustment, on the same level as that required following the death of a loved one or a bitter divorce? When I began asking friends and acquaintances if they had experienced this problem, I learned to my great surprise that many of them had suffered through a very difficult and painful period after retirement, particularly if the termination of their employment had not been of their own choosing but that of their employer. I also learned that most were embarrassed to talk about it because, in many people's minds, retirement is supposed to be a glorious time of freedom from stress and the normal demands of life.

This can be an especially dangerous time for recent retirees who are susceptible to making life-altering mistakes in an effort to alleviate the emotional tension they are experiencing, such as selling one's house and moving to a new location, buying a second home, making poor investments, divorcing, or self medicating with alcohol or drugs.

As I continued to search for the source of my problem I began talking to more and more people about how they experienced the transition to retirement. I discovered most of those who encountered the greatest difficulty had enjoyed very successful careers and suffered from achievement addiction. During their careers they received a great deal of positive rewards (monetary and emotional) because they were very good at their jobs. Over the years they began to need this positive feedback as an essential aspect of their existence. In effect, a large part of their identities were job-related. They defined themselves by what they did, not who they were as people. So for them, retirement represented a subconscious loss of their sense of self.

I immediately realized this was the primary cause of my emotional distress. A very large part of my identity was being the CEO and chairman of the company I founded. I saw everything through the prism of the business, and what I needed to do to ensure its success. Over time my very identity became infused with the role I played running the business. I did not see myself as a person independent from what I did for a living — it had defined me.

I noticed that during my own faltering attempts to adjust to retirement, many of the newly experienced marital irritations and frustrations I experienced were caused by a condition I call "marital compression". This is a situation whereby two married people who were accustomed to spending ten to twelve hours a day apart, five days a week for many years, suddenly find themselves thrust together each and every day. As we will learn later in the book, this sudden increase in togetherness often intensifies the irritation and annoyance caused by personality type conflicts, thus highlighting and aggravating areas of incompatibility that were lying dormant for years. It's one thing to argue with your spouse while cooking Sunday dinner, but try working in the kitchen together every day. Sunday may be manageable because tomorrow you go back to work, but how do you escape the source of the conflict if it presents itself multiple times a day, or several times a week?

Early Family Influences

Let's examine a few additional sources of conflict, beginning with early family influences. Our first example is the life orientation of a child raised within a large and loving family where unconditional positive regard was the order of the day. Holidays were festive occasions filled with good cheer, laughter, play and positive energy. As a result the child grows up to view family and holidays as wonderfully positive experiences that offer love, good will and emotional support. Let's call this person Mr. or Ms. Lucky. Then along comes Mr. or Ms. Right and a strong bond is established.

But Right did not experience the same type of upbringing. This individual was raised by a family that was much more austere, distant and ambivalent toward the child. Most of the time this person was more or less ignored during family gatherings and the atmosphere was poisoned by arguments, criticisms and negative energy. As an adult Right, at best, establishes a neutral opinion regarding family gatherings, though most likely these occasions do not engender positive emotions, but rather they understandably raise anxiety and defensive behavior. Right and Lucky go on to marry, and Lucky wants to live close to the warm and loving family that offered such positive experiences while growing up. Uh oh! While Lucky loves to be close to family members, Right wants nothing to do with them. When Right is dragged kicking and screaming to family gatherings, anger, resentment and feelings of alienation may result.

Financial resources are another early family difference that often cause conflict. Imagine a spouse who was raised with a mindset that money would always be more than sufficient to meet life's requirements coupled with one who was raised in a family that struggled to make ends meet. One partner believes money is an abundant resource, while the other thinks it is elusive, difficult to obtain and must be hoarded to ensure security. One spouse has an expansive view of money while the other sees it more as a scarcity. Unless resolved, these differences in perspective can be a constant source of irritation and disagreement within the marriage.

There are many other potential conflicts caused by early family influences; the important point is that these beliefs and tendencies are rooted deeply within us. They are difficult to modify because they are essential aspects of early childhood experience, and thus strong elements of core belief systems in adulthood.

Repressed Emotions

Another source of potential conflict is repressed emotion. Few of us were raised in an idyllic setting where mother catered to our every physical and emotional need. Rather, we came into the world and had many of our early needs met, but most likely many were not. If we were fortunate enough to be born into a loving and caring family with attentive parents we grew into healthy adults possessing few deep-seated emotional conflicts; however, if we were less fortunate we entered into a more tumultuous environment where our trust in the benevolent flow of life was damaged in some way.

Effective parenting is challenging because adults carry within them the psychological pain they incurred during childhood and inflict it, for better or worse, onto their children. They usually aren't aware of the damaging nature of their parenting because they are simply functioning in accordance with the psychological pattern embedded within them. Parents with acute emotional issues lose some of their capacity to feel in general and can therefore become insensitive to the emotional needs of their children, particularly when it comes to providing desperately needed love and nurturance. The product of this type of parenting is usually a child who enters adulthood with more than a few emotional contradictions.

We can see the emotional pain we carry with us from childhood is deeply buried in our subconscious, and can result in hidden land mines in our relationships. Life will be proceeding normally when all of a sudden, an emotional flare up that defies logic occurs.

Norma was raised in a family of three; she was the middle child with a sweet disposition and a reserved personality. During her childhood she felt overlooked and discounted and was not given as much consideration from her father and classmates as she needed. At times she was made to feel transparent and irrelevant. She felt as though her wants and desires did not matter. This happened repeatedly throughout her childhood.

Time passed; she married and one lovely summer evening there was a family gathering at her home. After dinner she decided dessert was needed and left for the supermarket. During her absence the group appeared to be getting restless and her husband decided to start a game of charades that had been planned for the evening's entertainment, not considering that it would be a problem for his wife. When she returned and saw the game had begun without her, she flew into a rage and began screaming at her husband in front of all in attendance, completely embarrassing him. This was totally out of character for her, but symptomatic of what happens when a specific and unique set of circumstances trigger deep-seated emotional pain: loss of control and a reaction far in excess of the circumstances that caused it.

In marriages these emotional trigger points may lie dormant, unleashed only when the right set of circumstances arises. Once activated, an excessive emotional reaction usually occurs. If you have ever said things to your spouse like, "You're acting like a maniac," "Get a hold of yourself," "What the hell is wrong with you?" — and my favorite — "You need to see a shrink!" you have most likely experienced one or more of these episodes. Raymond Hull sums up the problem with the observation, "All marriages are happy. It's the living together afterward that causes all the trouble."[4]

The better a person's mental health, the fewer of these trigger points are embedded in the psyche. An individual may have a few large areas of encapsulated pain possessing high amounts of compressed energy, or several smaller pressure point areas. However, the psychological dynamics

---

[4] ThinkExist.com, 2010

at play between partners have great bearing and influence on the overall happiness of the marriage and can become a major source of repressed anger and resentment.

Body Dominant Versus Brain Dominant

People don't all share the same way of being in the world. I am not talking about personality type, but about how one is anchored, or the manner in which one prefers to experience life. Some people like to accomplish things with their bodies, such as exercising, golf, tennis, fishing, swimming, running, hiking and biking. These people are body dominant types who feel centered and refreshed whenever they use their bodies in a highly physical way. Given their preferences, they would rather be involved in some type of physical activity than engage in more sedentary pursuits. They enjoy the challenge of sports because it infuses energy and enjoyment into their lives and brings them together with others who share their body orientation. The `Over 60' marathons are a good example of body dominant people who endorse this lifestyle well into their later years. Of course, body dominant people may enjoy reading and thinking as well, but these are not their predominant ways of being, or preferred sources of satisfaction.

It is easy to mislabel this type because body dominant types often experience physical activity vicariously. If you watch them carefully, you'll find they enjoy following a wide variety of sports on TV. I am not talking about merely following a favorite team; I mean most all sports draw their attention. Also, you will notice they enjoy action-adventure movies that provide a simulated physical experience. Many of these types participated in, and often excelled at, sports when they were young.

An alternative human orientation is one of brain dominance. These people would rather be reading, thinking, analyzing or learning than participating in activities of a physical nature. You will find them in libraries, book clubs, science fairs, chess clubs, computer groups, writers' workshops and on the Internet. When the opportunity for strenuous exercise arises they think, "What's the point?"

Whenever brain dominant people use their minds vigorously, it is relaxing and pleasurable for them. They would rather work a crossword puzzle or engage in a stimulating discussion than go hiking, jogging or biking. Thinking is a primary source of pleasure for them and they can spend endless hours in a bookstore just anticipating all the adventures waiting to be experienced inside the covers of each book. These people may enjoy physical activities as well, but such are not their preferential or primary ways of functioning.

If partners in a marriage share a similar orientation, they enjoy doing the same things together. There is less friction associated with their choice of activities, exemplified in the example of a spouse stating, "Honey, let's go on a five-mile hike through the Great Gorge Nature Preserve this weekend," and receiving the response, "Great, let's do it!" Can you imagine, however, what will happen if a body dominant spouse makes the very same statement to a brain dominant partner? The answer would most likely be, "Are you crazy?! Why in the world would I want to do that?"

When you imagine a good day in your life, what are you doing: using your brain or your body? Would your spouse experience the same level of joy from the activities you selected? If not, your partner could often be involved in activities that are not as enjoyable or enriching as they are for you. I often think the reason that watching movies is so enjoyable to many partners with different orientations is that movies provide both a simulated physical experience and mental stimulation, thus providing something enjoyable for all.

I recently spoke to a retired couple that possessed dissimilar orientations and had been married for forty-five years. The husband was body dominant and the wife was brain dominant. When I asked them to describe a typical day I learned they spent a great deal of time apart, he exercising at the club, biking and being outdoors while she stayed home and read books, perused the Internet and watched cooking shows on TV. Each made accommodations for the interests of the other, but there was acknowledgement that conflict and tensions occasionally arose when planning shared activities.

By identifying body/brain preferences in your marriage, you can take steps to avoid any stress caused by dominance disparities.

Personality Type

By far the largest ongoing source of conflict within a marriage is the interaction between distinct personality types. The personality represents a full expression of a person's identity. Unlike family influences and mental health, which are variables that could be managed by taking explicit actions and making specific compromises, the personality type is all-encompassing in a relationship. It touches every point of contact between spouses at all times. It represents a clear and direct expression of the enduring qualities, or essence, of each person. Except in jest, seldom do you hear someone say, "You should change your personality." The reason is that it is not possible. The best one can hope for is progress in the attainment of greater health within the confines of one's existing personality.

Personality type conflicts can be extremely frustrating in a marriage; there seems to be no way to effectively deal with them because they are created by two people expressing their own unique qualities. Many people try to resolve these exasperating clashes by creating distance from the spouse, thinking that if they limit the time spent together the opportunity for conflict to erupt will be reduced. This is usually not a good long-term solution; creating distance solves nothing and often leaves a marriage anemic and much less satisfying.

I once had a recent retiree tell me she understood what an oyster felt like. When I asked her what she meant she said, "One grain of sand can create a lot of irritation and it takes a very long time for it to turn into a pearl." I have known couples who have suffered recurring conflicts over the same issues for decades simply because they had no way of resolving their differences. Over time these couples resign themselves to the inevitability of periodic anger and frustration and try to manage their lives around it – but it never goes away. Neither partner has the insight or personal power to alter the conflicted nature of the relationship because its origins stem from the intrinsic nature of their personalities and the innate expression of their identities. I believe this is one of the reasons for

Thoreau's statement, "The mass of men lead lives of quiet desperation."[5]

These conflicts are often supercharged when one partner possesses a more forceful personality and uses anger and confrontation to dominate the relationship. The issue of dominance and control is an age-old problem, and is the focal point of Woody Allen's humorous statement, "In my house I am boss. My wife is just the decision-maker."[6]

In high conflict situations, the less dominant spouse usually responds in one of the following ways: (1) relents and goes along, feeling resentment; (2) relents and then responds with passive aggression; (3) creates as much distance from the dominant partner as possible. None of these responses are healthy for the relationship over the long term. Options 1 and 2 are self-esteem killers and Option 3 is merely an act of self-preservation.

Now that we have explored some of the common sources of conflict in relationships, let's learn about the unexpected role the heart plays in our love relationships.

---

[5] *Walden,* Henry David Thoreau, Boston, Beacon Press, Chapter 1: Economy, pg. 6, 2004

[6] InnocentEnglish.com

Chapter 2

Listening to Your Heart

I would rather have eyes that cannot see; ears that cannot hear; lips that cannot speak; than a heart that cannot love.

— *Robert Tizon*

There are only two ways to exist in the world: giving love or asking for love – that's it. Even when you witness people doing stupid and terrible things, if you really knew what was going on inside of them, they are really asking for love in some convoluted way. Deeply understanding this one concept has the power to change your life because it prevents your mind from conjuring all sorts of reasons and logic for people's behavior: "He's mean, insensitive and over controlling," "She's cold, distant and uncaring." See what I mean? When we project these beliefs onto the other person we then respond with deep anger or defensiveness as if our thoughts represented truth in the absolute. Conflict and misunderstanding then ensue, and your relationship ends up in a twist. It takes courage and a leap of faith to give love to someone who has hurt you. This is not true however if, at the very core of your being, you realize the person, in some disguised and obscure way, is asking for love, needs love and wants love, but doesn't know how to go about it and is acting out in some foolish or hurtful way.

A common misconception about love is that it is a weak or feeble emotion. Nothing could be further from the truth. An act of love is the most powerful force on Earth. The reason is that every act of love is a projection of a force field with divine origins. It is our link to the divine power that flows through the heart. If you pay close attention to your heart when you are expressing pure love you can feel it emanating from the heart outward. It feels all-encompassing. So it is a big mistake to underestimate the power of love to transform your relationships.

Because the essence of life is very simple, either giving or asking for love, we need to learn about the origins of love and the intricate role it plays in our relationships. There are so many erroneous notions about love, we must start from the beginning and learn the essential role the heart plays in our love relationships.

Your Unique Heartprint

We have always known intuitively that the heart plays a role in our emotions, and demonstrate this instinct with statements such as, "He broke my heart," or "My heart reached out to her." But little do most of us know the powerful role the heart plays in helping us manage our lives. More than just a pump that moves our blood throughout the body, the human heart has been shown through research to be a complex organism with its own purposeful "brain". There are approximately 40,000 neurons in the human heart which are identical to those found in the human brain, and compose fifty percent of the heart's mass. These cells produce a strong electromagnetic field that radiates out from the heart. Joseph Chilton Pearce states that heart cells produce two and a half watts of electrical energy with each pulsation, with amplitude forty to sixty times greater than that of brain waves. This electromagnetic (em) field radiates out about twelve to fifteen feet from the body, with the strongest part of the field concentrated within a radius of approximately three feet.[7]

---

[7] Joseph Chilton Pearce, *The Biology of Transcendence,* Park Street Press, Rochester, Vermont, 2002.

The heart is constantly communicating with the brain, body and world in general, and chooses the information it needs to operate effectively. It is constantly exchanging information through its em field in an attempt to optimize experience. The "heart brain" enables it to learn, retain, and make decisions independent of the brain. Often it is aware of circumstances in the environment before the brain awakens to them. Research at the Institute of Heartmath shows that the information the heart continuously forwards to the brain influences the higher brain's decision making, including its emotional processing.

The em field radiating from our hearts represents our own unique heartprint. Each heartprint is unique and "one of a kind." Every beat of our heart carries complex messages that affect our emotions, physical health and quality of life we experience.

The Power of Love

One person's heart signal can affect another's brainwaves when they come into contact. Love is more than an emotion; it is an electromagnetic phenomenon. Donna Karan, the well-known fashion designer has described this unusual influence when speaking of her close friendship with the spiritual teacher Deepak Chopra, "From the moment <we> met I knew there was a connection, and you can't explain that connection. It's just something that was there and I think you call it energy or call it something from a past life – call it karma."[8] When someone is addressing you from a place of love, your heart feels it and responds by sending positive signals throughout your body. When the electromagnetic current is negative, filled with anger and strong negative emotions the heart responds by withdrawing in a defensive fashion.

When you meet a new person an exchange of information occurs through commingled em fields. A great deal of nonverbal information is exchanged by a hug, dance or a conversation in a very short period of time. Let me give you an example.

Think back to your single days, when you were dating; did you ever go out with a very attractive boy or girl only to feel repelled by the person for no apparent reason? Have you ever walked down the street and observed a very unappealing looking man with a complete knockout on his arm (or vice versa)? Did you ever wonder what that "beautiful person" saw in that seemingly unattractive individual? The answer is coherence in their energy fields.

------

[8] *Mindmeld,* Katherine Rosman, WSJ, Issue 10, September 2010, pgs. 19-20.

By this I mean that, when they met and exchanged information through their individual heartprints, there was coherence, or a transpersonal connection characterized by unity and compatibility. In other words, they are in sync, on the same wavelength, in the groove and simpatico on a deep level.

Doc Childre, the author of *The Heartmath Solution,* describes incoherence being similar to light particles that are diffuse and spinning around in a disorderly fashion. When these very same light particles move into coherence they become transformed into an incredibly powerful laser beam. Similarly, when two people function in coherence, everything is aligned and moving in harmony within their relationship. This includes the organs in their bodies and emotions being felt and shared. It is a very powerful and transformative effect.

When heartprint information is exchanged, it is not trivial in nature but contains the most intimate kind of information that is outside the awareness of either individual, such as spiritual evolution, trustworthiness, loyalty, empathy, sensitivity and overall life orientation. When a love connection is made between two people, all of this information locks into place and creates a strong attractor field composed of positive emotions. These emotions have the power to affect a person's breathing, heart rate, and blood pressure and generate "I can't live without you" feelings.

This information gets sent to the brain not as a laundry list of traits or characteristics but as an intuitive feeling of magnetic attraction, which is experienced as a 'go' signal. The longer two people are together the more they learn about one another on a nonverbal level through information exchange in their respective energy fields. It goes on continuously. This process does not only occur in love relationships, but in social interactions as well. Your heartprint functions as a satellite dish tuned to the em fields of those you encounter, sending and receiving nonverbal information and then routing it to the brain and back again.

The Heart Chakra

In ancient Hindu texts the heart chakra is described as being a nexus point of energy located in the center of the chest and the domain of human intimacy. It is considered essential to affection, warmth, nurturing, friendship and familiarity. When it has been fully opened, it becomes the channel for universal love: what the Buddhists call "The Great Compassion" and Christians call "Christ Consciousness." It is believed that divine energy is able to work through this center once it is open. This is probably why, in so many cultures, the heart is said to be the seat of the soul.

This chakra enables you to feel joy, unity, laughter and especially love. It expands your capacity to be generous, sensitive, forgiving and tolerant. It is generally considered the most important energy center in your psyche, because it is from this chakra that love emanates. It is naturally associated with family, partners, friends, spiritual family members and animals. When it is balanced, you care about how you affect others. You want to touch them in a positive, nurturing way.

A well-balanced heart chakra will inspire your highest ideals and desires, and leave you feeling positive and nurturing. In your body, this chakra governs the heart, circulation, breasts, and arteries. The heart chakra vibrates and expresses the sentiments of caring, compassion and love.

When your heart chakra is balanced, you accept yourself and others in a non-judgmental way. You recognize beauty in yourself and others while overlooking weaknesses. It is because of a balanced heart chakra that you can be kind and forgiving, as well as quick to pardon. You experience an overall lightness of being.

If your heart chakra is off balance or shut down, you might have a tendency to reject intimacy. You might even intentionally push otherwise loving and lovable people away from you. Without this sense of connection, you become critical, suspicious and defensive. Paranoia becomes a real possibility. If your heart center shuts down completely, you may be inclined toward secrecy, betrayal and addictions.

By closing your heart you distance yourself from others, who in turn reject you, creating a vicious circle that seems to validate your decision to seal yourself off. Again and again you withdraw. Again and again you're rejected. It's a self-fulfilling prophecy. Your heart becomes more closed and you become more isolated. This can cause mental illness and physical disease.

The Heart and Marriage

Unless you married because your hormones were in overdrive, or you liked her high cheekbones or his Ferrari, you made a heart connection with your spouse. The only way it would be possible not to make this connection would be if you discounted your intuition and what your heart was telling you during your courtship. If you made your marriage decision based on ego attachments such as beauty, money, power or prestige and possibly financial security without a strong heart connection, chances are your relationship is unfulfilling—or you may be divorced and on to your second or third marriage. The reason is that these traits are not sufficient in and of themselves to sustain a long-term relationship such as marriage because they are not durable over time and lack substance.

When the energy fields have coherence between two individuals, it means that on a very broad scale across critically important and very personal dimensions, you are fundamentally and permanently compatible, unless one or both of the parties change in basic character across a wide spectrum, which is unlikely but not impossible. If coherence were not achieved during the courtship stage your heart would have sent strong messages to your brain to exit the relationship. In fact, you would have growing feelings of repulsion that would be intolerable to you emotionally over time. So we can see that, in most marriages, the fundamental building blocks have been put in place to resolve conflicts and continuously evolve and improve the marriage, provided the relationship was based on more than superficial attributes. This view is supported by Deepak Chopra: "However good or bad you feel about your relationship, the person you are with at this moment is the 'right' person because he or she is the mirror of who you are inside."[9]

I know what you are thinking: what happens if you feel you have only partial coherence, and overlooked some aspects of your partner that are now causing conflicts in your marriage? Good question, and what the remainder of this book is about. You can have coherence and yet suffer periodic conflicts in your marriage. The main point is that sufficient coherence was most likely attained or the relationship could not have progressed to the point of marriage, unless one or both parties lacked any sense of self-awareness. This coherence is what can be relied upon to resolve differences and elevate your marriage to a higher and more satisfying plane.

The Heart and the Divine Energy Field

The heart is the first organ created in utero. No one understands why it starts beating; it just commences in accordance with some pre-established level of cellular growth or biological spark. It is important to note the brain is not the first organ of growth, but the heart. As discussed

---

[9] *The Art of Romantic Relationships,* Discovery of Your Potential, Miramar, Florida, 2009

previously, the Heart Chakra has always been considered our spiritual center because love is of the spirit and not of the mind.

In my previous book, *The Retiring Mind: How to Make the Psychological Transition to Retirement,* I describe the notion of a divine energy field. You can call it the Holy Spirit, Tao, Buddha Mind or Brahman; it makes no difference. I call it the divine energy field because the term transcends any particular religion or belief system. This field effect is divine by nature, meaning it does not come from man or this plane of existence. It follows a nonlinear trajectory and moves based on its own, higher-order intelligence. Its only expression is love and its only product is goodness. It is contacted through prayer, meditation, music and contemplation. Its passageway is the heart. This is important because the essence of spirituality is a strong sense of purpose in life and deep feelings of connectedness within, to others and to spirit, which is a form of higher power.

I previously mentioned I consider marriage to be sacred. Possibly now you can understand why I hold this belief. The heart plays a pivotal role in the establishment of love relationships. We are the only beings that make love face-to-face and thus heart to heart. The heart field coherence between a mother and child is absolutely essential for healthy brain development, the emergence of consciousness and the development of a sense of loving trust within the infant. This occurs when positive emotions, such as expressions of love, tenderness, happiness, touch and appreciation, are shared and extended to the infant by the mother. These patterns are imprinted on the heart and brain of the child and remain there for an entire lifetime. Love is a divine expression that is sent from the heart and is received by the heart.

The implications of this heart connection are immense. In essence, the most important component we put into our love relationships is not what we do or say but what we are: our overall inner orientation, such as ideas, beliefs, consciousness level, psychological profile and evolutionary pattern. This also points us in the direction of personal growth as a promising path that may lead to greater intimacy and harmony within our relationships.

It is now time for you to identify your personality type. In the chapter that follows you will be employing the Enneagram to help identify your unique personality type. If you have read my previous book, *The Retiring Mind: How to Make the Psychological Transition to Retirement*, and have successfully identified your E-Type, you may skip this chapter and go on to Chapter 4: Identifying and Resolving E-Type Conflicts.

Chapter 3

Identifying Your E-Type

Some people come into our lives and quickly go.
Some stay for a while and leave footprints on our
hearts. And we are never, ever the same

— *Flavia Weedn*

I first discovered the Enneagram in the late 1980s when I read the book *The Enneagram: Understanding Yourself and the Others in Your Life* by Helen Palmer. I recall being very impressed by the depth of knowledge provided by this system for describing personality types. During my graduate studies in psychology, I was exposed to every type of analysis one can imagine. There were times when I felt like a lab rat because I completed so many psychological questionnaires that described my personality. As a result of those experiences, I thought I knew myself rather well—until I started studying the Enneagram. I discovered that it brought my self-knowledge to a higher and more comprehensive level.

I know the Enneagram Types (E-Types) of all of my family members and have used this extremely powerful tool throughout my business career. It has particularly helped me to better understand my wife and where our differences manifest in our relationship. It has always provided valuable information and increased my self-understanding as well as that of my close associates.

As a first step, let's identify your E-Type. Please be aware that there is much more to the Enneagram methodology than you will learn in this book. We are going to be very pragmatic and use it primarily to increase your self-understanding and that of your spouse, as well as to gain insight into how the two of you interrelate. I have listed references in the Recommended Reading section at the end of the book if you care to learn more about the Enneagram.

The Enneagram

The Enneagram has a rather mysterious history. There are some who believe it was created by the Sufis as part of their esoteric oral tradition and revealed to the world by the Armenian mystic George Gurdjieff. Others believe Oscar Ichazo, a Bolivian psychotherapist who founded the Arica

School in Chile, conceived it. Ichazo most likely integrated the Sufi wisdom he garnered during his travels throughout Asia into a more formal model for understanding personality. A circular diagram on which personality types are symbolically represented at nine points around the circumference characterizes the Enneagram. Arrows reveal the personality types, their adjoining influences, and interconnections with other types.

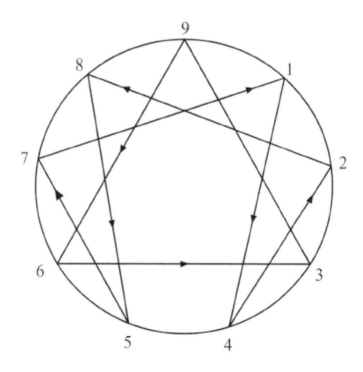

The Enneagram

Each E-Type is represented as functioning along a continuum somewhere between health (integration) and neurosis (disintegration). Although each of us possesses some of the characteristics of all nine types within us, through our genetics and early environment we have chosen to adopt one of the types for our primary pattern of behavior. Your E-Type reveals the underlying propensities that guide and influence your behavior. In the majority of instances I have witnessed, these behavioral descriptions come as somewhat of a surprise to those first learning their E-Type. In summary, the Enneagram enables you to gain knowledge of your true self, exposing the hidden motivations for actions and illusions you employ in your daily life.

The Formation of Type

You entered this world and were introduced to a large number of influences and circumstances that fluctuated and varied. Life was already well underway with the routine of your mother and other caregivers. You were integrated into this moving and shifting environment and had to adapt to the reality you encountered. All you knew at the time was that you had primal needs such as touch, food, interaction, and love that had to be met. You were helpless to satisfy your own needs and were completely dependent upon those around you for your care. When you felt this loving care it brought you immense joy and satisfaction, but most importantly, you felt secure.

As time went on and your needs continued to be satisfied, you gained confidence in the world around you, believing it was trustworthy and benevolent. In addition, you gained confidence that you could control your little world because when you cried someone came to feed, change, or hold you. You were never abandoned or neglected in any way and so you grew into a resilient, strong, and healthy adult. If this describes your early childhood, consider yourself blessed, because these consistently positive conditions are extremely rare.

How do people raised in a highly responsive and supportive setting see the world? What do they need? Abraham Maslow, the famed psychologist, performed the definitive study on this type of person. Dr. George Boeree, Professor of Psychology at Shippensburg University, lists the following needs as stated by these self-actualized individuals:

> **Truth**, rather than dishonesty
> **Goodness**, rather than evil
>
> **Beauty**, not ugliness or vulgarity

Unity, wholeness, and transcendence of opposites, not arbitrariness or forced choices

Aliveness, not deadness or the mechanization of life

Uniqueness, not bland uniformity

Perfection and necessity, not sloppiness, inconsistency, or accident

Completion, rather than incompleteness

Justice and order, not injustice and lawlessness

Simplicity, not unnecessary complexity

Richness, not environmental impoverishment

Effortlessness, not strain

Playfulness, not grim, humorless drudgery

Self-sufficiency, not dependency

Meaningfulness, rather than senselessness

These needs may seem perfectly normal to a self-actualized individual, but they aren't standard for everyone. The primary reason for this is that a person needs to trust the workings of the universe or divine flow of life to be sensitive to, and attracted to, these needs. If you went into the ghettos of major cities and asked those you encountered what they needed for happiness, I doubt many of these items would be mentioned. If people are struggling for survival or down on their luck, other needs take precedence.

Another key attribute of these self-actualized individuals is their calm acceptance of life. They do not fight with the world around them, but tend to go along with life's momentum and flow with the current of unfolding events. I point this out because these individuals seldom become achievement addicts for the simple reason that they move with the flow of divine energy and have no deeply embedded needs driving them to conquer and achieve. If anything, they may appear passive and ascetic simply because they are happy people and do not make great demands on their immediate environments. Why work until midnight on a deal when you can listen to music or walk in the woods and be filled with ecstasy?

Truthfully, these are not the nation builders and top executives of the world. They already have what everyone else is striving for—inner peace supported by a strong spiritual connection to the divine.

Now that we know what perfection looks like—what does it mean for those lost souls blindly milling around in the dark? Remember, we construct our worldview during the first four to five years of our lives. What happens if our early environment was not perfect, if it had some kinks in it? Our parents had their own stresses and conflicts to manage when we entered their lives as infants. Our own mothers or fathers, who most likely have an imprint on their psyches from being raised by imperfect parents, may very well have handed down this legacy to us, for better or for worse. As a result, as a small child you may have been subjected to inconsistent or deficient nurturing.

If you were fortunate, your needs were mostly satisfied, but with wide variability; if you were less fortunate, you were raised in a state of constant deprivation. Based on the unique pattern of your early environment, you made a critical decision—you could not completely trust the world around you to fulfill your needs. You were forced to react to this early environment in order to secure your own welfare and protection. To quote A.H. Almaas in his book *Facets of Unity: The Enneagram of Holy Ideas*: "Without basic trust, we don't have trust in our nature and our inner resources, and in the universe that gave birth to us, is constantly supporting us, constantly providing for us, and will continue providing for us whatever we really need."[10]

---

[10] A. H. Almass, *Facets of Unity: The Enneagram of Holy Ideas*, Berkeley, California: Diamond Books, 1998, Page 30.

Without basic trust, you could not count on things working out, and were left feeling at a loss and insufficient. You had to make some personal adjustments because you lost confidence in the reliability of your caregivers. You could not always take your vital safety and security for granted—things were not automatically provided for you without effort on your part. When you looked out over your immediate circumstances you made the determination that you did not always get the love and attention you needed when you needed it. Rather than trusting in the divine flow (Holy Spirit, Tao, Buddha mind, universal consciousness), you had to make changes to make things right. At this point you lost your innocence. Without basic trust you became more reluctant to take risks; feelings of hopelessness arose, and you lost your ability to relax. Possibly you decided you had to withdraw or make it on your own. Life became work. You projected your understanding of life as you experienced it in childhood onto your adult world. This became your own unique code of conduct. Most importantly, you seriously weakened or severed your connection with the divine energy field, which is the primary source of true happiness.

This loss is not unique to you, but is the general human condition. Unless you are one of Maslow's self-actualized people, you experienced need deprivation to some degree.

The only variation is the extent of your deprivation in childhood and your specific decision of how best to cope with it. You had several behavioral alternatives available to you: (1) try to be perfect; (2) become more loving and attentive so that you receive more love and attention in return; (3) draw attention to yourself through your accomplishments; (4) become angry and complain; (5) withdraw emotionally and disconnect from the pain; (6) become cautious, fearful, and suspicious, and hunker down; (7) act out and attract attention; (8) become angry and demanding; or (9) fade into transparency and make no waves. The behavior you chose at that early age represents your E-Type.

Your particular type describes how you have chosen to be in the world. You formed your personality, possibly through trial and error, at a premature age in order to cope with the contingencies encountered in the early childhood environment. What was the best course of action for you to take? Your needs were simple and basic. You could either make every effort to get them met or withdraw and form a protective shield to minimize the hurt caused by deprivation. Your decision structured the general personality framework and architecture you now use to travel through life.

It is now time to identify your E-Type. What follows is a brief description of each of the nine personality types. Please read each one carefully and try to identify the E-Type that best describes you. Don't be concerned if you identify with more than one type. If you are uncertain after reading these descriptions do not despair, a questionnaire is provided in Appendix A to help you confirm your choice.

E-Type 1: The Master

You are a perfectionist at heart. You have great interest in detail and like to solve problems and fix things. Your cars are always spotless and polished, your shoes are shined, and your clothes are usually clean and pressed. You care about your appearance and like to be well groomed. You receive pleasure from improving things around you and take great pride in your mastery over those areas in your life that are important. You tend to be tense and have difficulty relaxing before you accomplish everything on your to-do list. You are always tinkering with things and have a deep understanding and appreciation of how things work.

You are attracted to professions, such as engineering, where you can design and build things. You are extremely meticulous and like to do everything yourself because no one can meet your high standards of perfection. You are not a good delegator.

You are very dependable, hardworking, and efficient, and view the world through rules and regulations. You are highly respectful of the authority figures in your life. You tend to be controlling and slightly rigid in your thinking. You are highly analytical and secretly feel superior because of your high standards. You can be excessively critical of yourself and others, domineering, extremely demanding, and angry, but you try hard to suppress it. You can rub people the wrong way. You resent others who get ahead without sacrifice and commitment. You seldom meet people who you believe are as capable as you. You have the capacity to experience great pleasure and satisfaction, particularly if you believe it is well earned. You have a tendency to overwork and devote too much time to your career. Unhappiness stems from your perspective that most things in your life require a great deal of effort and attention to be acceptable, including yourself.

E-Type 2: The Enchanter

To you, relationships are the most important thing in your life. You have the unique ability to get other people to like you, by basically changing yourself and becoming whatever is most acceptable to them. You intuitively know what to do and what to say to lure an unsuspecting person into a relationship. You are often the "power behind the throne" of authority figures. You are a warm, tender, and supportive person capable of great caring and empathy.

You make a wonderful and attentive spouse and friend. You are focused on feeling and you have a very romantic view of life. You may read romance novels to satisfy a vicarious need for more love and passion in your life. Others may see you as living in la-la land, not interested in or knowledgeable of current events, but you know every anniversary and birthday in your family by heart. You actively keep in touch with friends and family via e-mail, cards on special occasions, and phone conversations. You usually know everything that is going on, in detail, within your network of relationships. You like children and enjoy caring for and interacting with them.

You have a tendency to get your own way through manipulation and seduction. You often give to others with the hidden intent of getting something in return. This is usually an unconscious motive that surfaces when you feel that you give more than you receive. On these occasions you complain, become frustrated, and feel a sense of betrayal and resentfulness. Feelings of ungratefulness can be a common emotion. You have a stubborn streak that is unshakable and you do not like to deviate from routine. Control over others is achieved through your helpfulness. You can make yourself indispensable to those around you, which is a form of security, control, and power. One of your most important goals is to be needed by others. It is easy for you to be aware and sensitive to the needs of others, but you often struggle when trying to establish a clear understanding of your own needs. More than anything you value feelings of love, security, and romance.

E-Type 3: The Star

You are an individual with strong achievement motivation who gravitates toward leadership. You are charming, cheerful, optimistic, and action oriented. You work hard and assume leadership roles in order to win in a competitive world. Your primary motivation is to avoid failure and be a success. You exude feelings of confidence and well-being, which attracts others to you. You look and act like a winner.

If you are a housewife, you are the president of the garden club; if you are a businessperson, you are the CEO, senior executive or general partner of a firm. You usually earn a good living. You are image conscious and marketing oriented. You have the ability to influence others and have good intuition regarding how to succeed. You are easily identifiable because you are always striving and busy. Your calendar is full of meetings and commitments. You are always on the go and focused on the outside world. Meeting all of your commitments challenges you.

You seldom take the time to reflect, and when you do, it makes you uncomfortable. You are socially skilled, attract attention, and can become a performer when the occasion calls for it. You take your computer and cell phone with you on vacation and secretly find doing a deal or taking calls from the office more pleasurable than actually spending time with your family. You portray an idealized image to others by living in the right neighborhood, with good-looking, high-achieving children, and an attractive spouse. You are drawn to and value material success above everything else and surround yourself with friends and associates who share similar views.

Your self-worth depends more upon what you do than who you are, and you tend to be disconnected to your inner self. You can change into whatever you need to be in order to win. This chameleon-like quality can trouble you, and you may wonder if you are betraying yourself on some occasions. You can take an idea and move quickly and directly into action. You are willing to take on authority figures if required to make progress. You are efficient, precise in your actions, and totally committed to success; however, deep inside you are more dedicated to the process than the outcome. You enjoy the recognition associated with accomplishment, but more than anything, you want to be a winner.

E-Type 4: The Drama Queen

You live your life swinging between exhilaration and depression. You are elegant, stylish, and sensitive with a flair for the dramatic. You are passionate, impulsive, and subject to severe mood swings. You can be a sensual lover one minute and a disapproving critic the next. You have a profound artistic nature and often can be seen as a "tortured soul". Your feelings are highly sensitive and you can be hurt simply by a small glance or gesture. You feel rejection deeply.

You are devilish by nature and do not conform to authority unless it is of the highest order. You can be extremely interesting while at the same time maddening. You often feel like a victim of life and become morose and self-destructive. You are cynical by nature and have little faith in the goodness of others. You take on a "poor me" attitude and have a habit of rejecting whatever is easy to obtain.

Deep intimacy is threatening to you because it makes you feel inadequate, as though something inside of you is missing. You prefer to keep relationships at arm's length. You romanticize those you want to attract, and then reject them once their flaws become evident.

Your customary mood is one of melancholy. You actually enjoy music, movies, books, and plays that offer a degree of wistful sadness. You have a heightened sensitivity to other people's emotions and pain and can be highly supportive of them in crisis. You have a temperamental connection to intense emotion. You may have a deep commitment to religion, spirituality, and metaphysics.

You occasionally overwhelm others with your strong passions and emotional outbursts. You cannot seem to relinquish the depth of suffering. In this state you can be pessimistic, skeptical, somber, irritable, complaining, despondent, critical, bitter, self-defeating, and vain—and that's just for starters. You can also be extremely interesting, fun, passionate, unique, clever, sensual, erotic, and noble. Your inner life can be characterized as searching for something that is missing—a feeling of being disconnected or unable to grasp something that you desperately need—which manifests as emotional conflicts and vivid drama.

E-Type 5: The Solitary Mystic

Above all else you seek solitude. You live a life of independence and choose sovereignty over attachment. You may live in a remote area. You reject dependency on anyone or anything and will not work in an environment that is hostile, closely controlled, or artificial. You may be self-employed. If required, you can shrink your personal needs down to a minimalist lifestyle without viewing it as a significant sacrifice. You do not like having your time confiscated by obligations or other people's schedules.

You love to read, ponder abstract concepts, and think deeply about nature. You can investigate arcane topics and become an expert in those areas of interest with little or no contact with the outside world. You will often surprise people with the depth and breadth of your knowledge on particular subjects. You live mainly in your head and attempt to limit emotional involvement as much as possible. You seldom reveal personal information to strangers.

You have a few select friends that you value highly, provided they grant you the freedom to come and go. You usually share a special bond with these select individuals because you have special interests in common. You are exceptionally loyal to the few friends you treasure. You seldom require the spotlight and prefer to be the power behind the scenes.

You can be invaluable to authority figures because of your ability to detach and look at things in depth with objectivity. You are a great scholar, teacher, writer, or inventor, and tend to be attracted to subjects considered New Age, such as metaphysics. What others consider far out, you consider mainstream and common sense.

At both family and social gatherings, you tend to be uncomfortable and can't wait to depart. You seldom work the room but instead seek out an interesting person or make yourself cleverly invisible. You process your emotions in private and can enjoy reviewing social interactions after they have occurred in the privacy of your thoughts. You are not extemporaneous and prefer speaking on a topic once you have given it a great deal of thought. You may love pets because you receive affection without onerous expectations and emotional entanglements. You are indifferent to praise and recognition from others and maintain a detached perspective regarding most things in your life.

When you become angry, you are seldom confrontational; rather, you withdraw into a cold silence and sulk. You can maintain this icy silence longer than expected. Rather than resolve a conflict through dialogue and emotional expression, you think your way through it by analyzing and compartmentalizing the issue until it is completely understood and resolved in your mind. Only then are you capable of moving toward reconciliation.

In matters of money, you are apt to be very conservative and instinctively hoard your resources, so that your independence cannot be threatened. When you are engaged in work or social activities for an extended period of time, you require private time alone to recharge your batteries. You are rarely bored because of having nothing to do. There is so much to explore and learn. In a moment of honesty, you may admit feeling a sense of superiority over others because of the extent of your knowledge or because you need less than they do to be happy.

E-Type 6: The Closet Rebel

You are suspicious by nature and attracted to underdog causes. You work best in environments that are orderly, predictable, structured, and routine. You are cautious and socially inhibited but can exert tremendous energy on any project you believe in. You follow strong, compassionate leaders and can be extremely loyal to your employer, provided that fairness and honesty are practiced at all times. You are well known for having a good "BS detector," and you become very suspicious of those you believe are dishonest or hustlers.

You tend toward procrastination, particularly at the end of projects. When evaluating issues, you will identify everything that could go wrong without expressing confidence in the outcome. You are cynical by nature and can be characterized by H.L. Mencken's definition of a cynic, "A cynic is a man who, when he smells flowers, looks around for the coffin." You have a rebellious streak that often goes unnoticed by your friends and coworkers because you keep it well hidden from view.

You can be attracted to gurus, anti-establishment provocateurs, and those who resist conventional wisdom. Above all you want to feel safe and secure. You constantly monitor your immediate environment for anything that could be harmful. You are loyal, analytical, dutiful, precise, hardworking, punctual, and a good critical thinker and problem solver. You are particularly adept at identifying problems that could go wrong at the beginning of any venture.

You have problems submitting to authority and can become passive-aggressive when being challenged. You can only work for someone you trust. You may be attracted to self-employment, so that you can exert more control over authority relationships. You can frustrate loved ones with your skepticism and doubt regarding change and new initiatives. You are usually well informed on subjects that matter, and those close to you respect your opinion. What you need most is to align with a cause or organizational leader that is just and honorable.

E-Type 7: The Cruise Director

You are optimistic by nature and have an upbeat personality. You are charming and a terrific networker. People gravitate to you because of your charisma, bright outlook, and adventuresome demeanor. You like to go places and do things—the more the better. You look forward to fun-filled outings with much anticipation. You seldom feel the emotion of fear. Life is full of interesting possibilities and you want to partake in each and every one of them.

You keep multiple options open and are highly flexible in your approach to life. If something does not work out, you do not get depressed but simply shift over to another track of entertaining experience. You love Disney World. You have an active imagination and vivid fantasy life. You would make a terrific children's author, fiction novelist, salesperson, or real estate agent. You enjoy planning and hosting social events, such as birthdays and anniversaries.

You have good taste and enjoy sampling the best the world has to offer. You are a passionate traveler and have interesting memories and artifacts collected from romantic locales. You have visionary plans for the future that are extremely exciting.

You need to maintain high levels of stimulation because you can quickly lose interest if things are not fun and interesting. You are much better at visualizing, planning, and organizing a project than you are doing the day-to-day detailed work required for successful completion. You do not like to get bogged down in details and drudgery. You like to fly above the clouds and zoom in whenever the mood needs to be elevated.

You lift the spirits of those around you and help others see the possibilities in any situation. You believe that you can talk your way out of most difficult situations because you are charming and quick-witted. You do not like authority that is unreasonable and will quickly exit any environment that is too controlling, heavy-handed, or rule governed.

You have a weakness for overindulgence, and occasionally take on too much activity without anticipating the consequences. Under stress you become irritable, restless, and overconfident. At your worst you are self-indulgent. However, your moodiness does not last long because it is very easy for you to find new challenges and adventures. You do not do well with boring routine and excel in activities where there is freedom of movement, either physically or intellectually. Above all you need play.

E-Type 8: The Conquistador

You gravitate toward power and control. You have a need to take charge and be a leader. You are a natural at confronting obstacles and taking action. You can move mountains once you are committed to a goal. You are not particularly introspective, and few people really know your inner self. You see yourself as a protector of those less powerful or fortunate. You do not trust anyone who will not fight for his or her strongly held beliefs.

You are extremely comfortable with confrontation and believe that it is the most effective way to get at the truth. You are often not aware that others are intimidated by your behavior and dislike your direct approach. You do not respect weakness. You have an expanded sense of self and believe you are physically powerful. You believe that only the strong survive.

When you become angry you feel as though your body grows larger and more powerful. You will fight to the death in an argument and often weaken your opponents through sheer willpower. You seldom back down. You get into trouble when you become bored. You will pick a fight to make things interesting, or you will go to the extreme through excessive spending, overeating, binge drinking, or lustfulness.

You are predatory by nature and want to gain complete control over your environment. You like to break the rules to see what happens. You often function as if rules were made for other people. You flourish in the atmosphere of open competition. Seldom are others willing to sacrifice as much as you to win. You overcome barriers through sheer force of will. You feel secure only when you are calling the shots and in control.

You dislike injustice and will come to the aggressive defense of those being persecuted. You are softhearted toward friends and those in your sphere of influence. You tend to see things in terms of black and white. You seldom feel fear and become anxious only when you have not identified the weaknesses of your opponents.

You can become ruthless when you feel vulnerable. While you are functioning in your comfort zone most others around you can feel deeply threatened and stressed. If you were a toy you would be an action hero. If you were a TV personality you would be Bill O'Reilly. Your greatest weaknesses are insensitivity, impatience, self-centeredness, and hyperactivity. Most of all, you need a castle.

E-Type 9: The Harmonizer

You can clearly see both sides of any issue. You are a great friend and can listen and be very helpful in times of need.

You have good insight into the inner world of those close to you and are sought out for advice and counsel. You are an inherently good person, generous, kind, modest, contented, peaceful, humorous, and softhearted. You are dependable, stable, reliable, unpretentious, and nurturing. Most of all you are well balanced. You love animals and nature.

You are attracted to jobs that require attention to detail and structured routine. You excel in any position that requires you to put things into order, such as accounting and office administration. You thrive in a bureaucracy.

You are a supportive and loving spouse. You are a well-known procrastinator, easily diverted by trivial things and prone to lose sight of important tasks. You often put off a critical task to the end of the day and then forget about it.

You have difficulty saying no and struggle with decision-making. It is easier for you to help a friend make a decision than it is for you to know the best course of action for yourself. You can stay in a suspended state of uncertainty for a long time without making an important decision and taking appropriate action. You can become very stubborn when others try to help you with a decision.

You have a long list of rituals that function much like a narcotic, such as cleaning closets, endless hours of watching TV, and other acts of diversion. These obsessive activities are used to prevent you from addressing important life issues. An independent observer would say you spend all day on unimportant things and little or no time on matters that improve your life.

You have an over reliance on other people and leach their energy and ambition. You need friends and loved ones to initiate social activities so you can go along. You assimilate their interests and priorities into your life without considering your own needs and opinions. You are more of a follower than a leader. When you become angry you are passive-aggressive. You can hold grievances inside for a long period and then explode. On these rare occasions it feels good to finally make a strong statement on your own behalf.

You are weak-willed and often give up on resolving frustrations and conflicts until everything breaks down. This can lead to depression. You are overly sensitive to criticism and are lacking in self-confidence. You could be extremely handsome or beautiful and still feel insecure regarding your appearance. You are physically active but complacent by nature and lack focused energy. More than anything you need love and greater self-awareness.

At this point you have hopefully selected one of the E-Types and feel confident that it accurately describes your personality. You may not share all of the qualities described for your type due to the fact that very healthy individuals often have less of the negative and more of the positive qualities, while less healthy individuals frequently have more of the negative and perhaps less of the positive qualities. The type you have selected should describe you in general. Perhaps you are unsure which type best describes you. If so, please go to Appendix A and complete the E-Type Questionnaire. It will help you make your choice. Your true type should be included in your highest two or three scores.

If you remain unsure I suggest talking with your spouse, family members and close friends and asking for their opinion. You may be surprised at how well they know the real you. It is essential that your spouse select an E-Type as well. Do not continue on to the next chapter until you have both correctly identified your E-Type.

Chapter 4

Identifying and Resolving E-Type Conflicts

*True love is like a pair of socks: you gotta have two
and they've gotta match.*

— Author Unknown

Marriage can be defined as two separate entities possessing individualized and unique aspects that are conjoined for the purpose of coexistence in an optimum state of satisfaction. These relationships, however, can become fertile ground for conflict because of the widely varying and poignant ways personalities react when juxtaposed with other personality types. I agree with Schopenhauer when he states, "Almost all of our sorrows spring out of our relations with other people."[11]

The interpersonal complexities that often arise between husband and wife are so commonplace that marital strife has long been the butt of jokes, such as, "My wife suggested a book for me to read to enhance our relationship. It was titled, *Women are from Venus, Men are Wrong.*"[12]

The sources of conflict existent in the unique combination of your E-Types are not always active in your relationship and may lie dormant for long periods of time. They become activated when stress levels are increased due to some outside catalyst. The triggering event can be something large such as retirement, or something much more incidental such as time, family or social pressures.

Under normal conditions personality influences are felt as 'curved' energy projections, easily intermingling and flowing together with those of the partner; however, under stress these soft curvatures can become sharpened and angular and released as powerfully focused negative energy which emanates from the hidden core or dark side of the

---

[11] GoldenProverbs.com

[12] GoodQuotes.info/love-quotes

personality. When directed toward the partner, these energy projectiles of strong emotion can feel like punches to the gut – hurtful, mean spirited and damaging.

Not all conflicts arise so forcefully; they can slowly appear from chronic irritation that builds up over time, caused by irreconcilable aspects between personality types. For example, a fun loving, free spirited individual married to an over controlling perfectionist offers ample opportunity for persistent antagonism. These incompatible components of the relationship, if not effectively managed, feel like a slow and painful poisoning or smoldering irritation that is constantly present between the partners. This type of conflict can be experienced as a wearing down, or exhausting frustration, that is usually shoved deep into a subterranean area of the psyche, only to resurface again another day as feelings of, "I can't take it anymore."

These types of conflicts create defensive behavior on the part of those involved, depending upon the distinctive nature of the E-Types. One individual will respond by sulking, another will be confrontational and erupt in anger, while others will engage in avoidance behavior. Each E-Type ushers forth its own signature of entangled energies and each holds the potential to unknowingly create conflicts within the relationship.

The energy of the personality is all-encompassing and permeates every area of coexistence with the partner. For this reason, we are going to cross-reference your E-Type with that of your spouse and learn about the exclusive dynamics at play between you. Hopefully this matching process will accurately describe the general tenor of your relationship, identify areas of potential disagreement and offer suggestions for conflict avoidance or resolution.

Using the chart that follows, locate the E-Type combination for you and your spouse and then turn to the adjoining page. (For example, if your combined E-Type were 3/5 you would turn to page 124.) It is essential that you and your spouse openly discuss the relevancy of the information associated with your unique E-Type combination. The goal is to establish a consensus regarding how you plan to avoid the latent points of discord that may reside within your relationship, which are caused by the reciprocal interaction between your respective E-Types. After you have openly shared your views and discussed their implications, you may then proceed to Chapter 5: Between a Man and a Woman.

E-Type Combinations

1/1 pg. 78	1/2 pg. 81	1/3 pg. 83
1/4 pg. 86	1/5 pg. 88	1/6 pg. 91
1/7 pg. 93	1/8 pg. 95	1/9 pg. 98
2/2 pg. 100	2/3 pg. 103	2/4 pg. 105
2/5 pg. 107	2/6 pg. 110	2/7 pg. 112
2/8 pg. 115	2/9 pg. 117	3/3 pg. 119
3/4 pg. 121	3/5 pg. 124	3/6 pg. 126
3/7 pg. 128	3/8 pg. 131	3/9 pg. 133
4/4 pg. 136	4/5 pg. 138	4/6 pg. 141
4/7 pg. 143	4/8 pg. 146	4/9 pg. 148
5/5 pg. 151	5/6 pg. 153	5/7 pg. 156
5/8 pg. 158	5/9 pg. 160	6/6 pg. 163
6/7 pg. 165	6/8 pg. 168	6/9 pg. 170
7/7 pg. 173	7/8 pg. 175	7/9 pg. 177
8/8 pg. 180	8/9 pg. 182	9/9 pg. 185

E-Type Combination 1/1

Master ♥ Master

General Nature of Your Relationship

This can be a rather stressful combination because both partners possess identical personality profiles, which means that both the positive and negative aspects of the Master are enhanced rather than diluted by a combination with another type. This relationship is focused on achievement at a very high level; therefore the house or apartment is usually neat and clean, decorated beautifully, the color combinations are exquisite, the clothes are stylish and the cars immaculate. As a family unit you are willing to strive to maintain your standards and feel satisfaction when your expectations are met.

Primary Sources of Conflict

The conflict that occurs in this relationship can become very chronic because it is based on judgment and control issues. Failure to meet expectations, no matter how oblique, can result in bursts of anger and disappointment.

Constant judgment can be poisonous to a marriage because it is based on an evaluation of someone not measuring up and thus there is a continuous sense of lack, impoverishment or not being good enough. Another major source of conflict is the need for control, because the Master only feels emotionally secure when in control. This couple will suffer conflicts when doing things together because each desires to execute in very precise and meticulous fashion, possibly not in agreement with the approach of the partner. It is frustrating to both partners when judgments are made that nothing is ever good enough.

Recommended Courses of Action

It would be highly beneficial if this couple took a judgment holiday. For one day, make a commitment to avoid judging your partner in any way. Attempt to be mindful of your tendency toward harsh self-criticism as well. At the end of the day, sit down with your partner and share your views regarding the holiday. How did it go? If both believe it was a positive experience, try it again the next day and then the next. Never let severe judgment go unacknowledged or unchallenged. Also, it would be helpful to designate leadership and support roles for shared tasks and then alternate. "Today you call the shots and I will help you; tomorrow we switch."

There is a key question you should ask yourself whenever a conflict arises in your relationship, "Would this issue matter if I were in the woods, or to a three-year old?" Your answer to this question will help you to ascertain whether or not the source of the conflict is arising from vital life sustaining aspects of your relationship or from a more distant place defined by social or ego pressures? If your answer is yes, recognize that the conflict has the power to destroy your relationship if not resolved satisfactorily. If your answer is no, there is a good chance the conflict may be less serious and may require an alternative approach to resolution.

E-Type Combination 1/2

Master   Enchanter

General Nature of Your Relationship

This relationship is based on codependence; one spouse has dedication to the practicalities of life and strives for tangible achievement while the other focuses on emotions and relationships. While one spouse has intensity of purpose the other keeps the family connected to the outside world; one partner is focused on accomplishment while the other provides the support needed for the relationship to maintain equilibrium.

Primary Sources of Conflict

Conflicts arise in this relationship when one partner is totally dedicated to accomplishment and does not provide the attention required by the other partner. One partner needs the personal satisfaction of achievement while the other needs emotional support. One partner thinks, "You don't know how hard I have to work," while the other thinks, "You don't know how badly I need your attention."

Conflicts usually erupt in the form of anger from one partner, and as strong emotion and stubbornness on the part of the other.

Recommended Courses of Action

The differences that reside within this relationship can be used to provide significant benefits to both parties. The Master needs the loving support provided by the Enchanter to be happy, while the Enchanter needs the practicality and focused energy provided by the Master. Conflict arises whenever this relationship gets out of balance. When this occurs one partner is perceived as being cold and indifferent while the other seems overly needy and requiring too much attention. This family unit can be improved by increased sensitivity to the needs of both parties. A good action plan for the Master is: 1) make it a priority to show greater attention and affection to your spouse on a regular basis; 2) do not become so consumed by work that you lose your emotional connection to your spouse. Recommendations for the Enchanter are 1) realize that compromise is required and do not demand that you always have things your own way; 2) guard against using excessive helpfulness as a means of manipulation and control.

There is a key question you should ask yourself whenever a conflict arises in your relationship, "Would this issue matter if I were in the woods, or to a three-year old?" Your answer to this question will help you to ascertain whether or not the source of the conflict is arising from vital life sustaining aspects of your relationship or from a more distant place defined by social or ego pressures? If your answer is yes, recognize that the conflict has the power to destroy your relationship if not resolved satisfactorily. If your answer is no, there is a good chance the conflict may be less serious and may require an alternative approach to resolution.

E-Type Combination 1/3

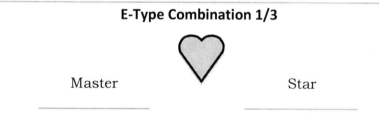

Master   Star

General Nature of Your Relationship

This is a high-octane relationship capable of extremely high accomplishment in almost any area. The house resonates with a whirling buzz of activity. Both partners are extremely energized to achieve their goals and will work around the clock if that is what it takes to succeed. One partner is highly detailed and orderly while the other usually functions as the `front person' of the relationship. Both partners intrinsically and naturally provide the necessary energy and support required for the recognition and success of the other. This is a 'most likely to succeed' connection.

Primary Sources of Conflict

One spouse's perspective is highly detailed and analytical while the other projects a model image. There is such high dedication to making progress and winning at all times that conflicts occur. On these occasions Masters want to delve deeply and comprehensively into the relationship and discuss all the details surrounding the cause of the conflict, while the Star wants to acknowledge the problem, promise to do better and move on without all the introspection. Stars react strongly when their self-image is being attacked, while Masters respond with anger when they are accused as being wrong. Because both partners can be strong willed and accustomed to prevailing in disagreements, these conflicts may not be thoroughly resolved, ending with the dispute being swept under the rug only to erupt later at inopportune times over trivial matters.

Recommended Courses of Action

This is a power couple with high energy and extreme focus. The cause of recurring conflicts needs to be identified and a structured plan of resolution established. This couple perceives the world from different perspectives, one truth seeking, and the other quick action. The best course of mediation is somewhere in the middle. This couple needs to plan for more down time to simply enjoy life together.

There is a key question you should ask yourself whenever a conflict arises in your relationship, "Would this issue matter if I were in the woods, or to a three-year old?" Your answer to this question will help you to ascertain whether or not the source of the conflict is arising from vital life sustaining aspects of your relationship or from a more distant place defined by social or ego pressures? If your answer is yes, recognize that the conflict has the power to destroy your relationship if not resolved satisfactorily. If your answer is no, there is a good chance the conflict may be less serious and may require an alternative approach to resolution.

E-Type Combination 1/4

Master   Drama Queen

General Nature of Your Relationship

This is a combustible relationship that mixes cold logic with emotional drama. The Master is logical and analytical by nature while the Drama Queen is full of passionate energy. While one spouse thinks, "Get control of yourself," the other thinks, "Why don't you ever let yourself go?" Each secretly functions as a 'shadow self' of the other, helping to bring out deep-seated aspects of both personalities. While one spouse brings order and routine to the marriage, the other brings drama, art and passion.

Primary Sources of Conflict

Conflict is experienced in this relationship when the moods of one partner are countered by the cold-blooded logic of the other, with one partner introducing feelings into the relationship while the other brings a more aloof perspective. Where one partner needs the drama of romance, the other needs a sense of proportion: where one partner needs heartfelt actions the other needs politeness and decorum.

Recommended Courses of Action

Oddly, the range of life experiences of both spouses is expanded in this combination. While one partner provides security and stability the other provides the unexpected and illogical, which adds spice to the relationship. A deeper and more insightful understanding on the part of both individuals will benefit this partnership. The Master needs to restrain the tendency to criticize, acknowledging that it erodes the self-esteem of the partner. The Drama Queen needs to realize that emotional displays appear illogical to the partner. There is potential for deep love and commitment embedded within this relationship, albeit dependent upon the sensitivity to the needs and expressions of both partners.

There is a key question you should ask yourself whenever a conflict arises in your relationship, "Would this issue matter if I were in the woods, or to a three-year old?" Your answer to this question will help you to ascertain whether or not the source of the conflict is arising from vital life sustaining aspects of your relationship or from a more distant place defined by social or ego pressures? If your answer is yes, recognize that the conflict has the power to destroy your relationship if not resolved satisfactorily. If your answer is no, there is a good chance the conflict may be less serious and may require an alternative approach to resolution.

E-Type Combination 1/5

Master · Solitary Mystic

General Nature of Your Relationship

This relationship can look remote and detached on the surface because both partners enjoy a cerebral existence. The Master loves problem solving and fixing things and functions from an analytical perspective; The Solitary Mystic can be more philosophical and conceptual and becomes excited by new ideas and concepts. Neither partner likes to have his or her personal space invaded and both can function independently for long periods of time.

Primary Sources of Conflict

Conflict between these partners usually occurs as a result of one or both partners becoming remote from the other. On these occasions the Master expresses anger while the Solitary Mystic responds with detachment. Often conflicts will occur and be ignored because neither wants to expend the energy to engage in open hostilities. Usually one partner will want to move directly toward a solution while the other wants to withdraw and mentally process the situation. Grudges can be held for very long periods of time. It is not until both parties seriously engage in conflict resolution that normality returns to the relationship.

Recommended Courses of Action

This couple has different styles of responding to conflict, with one partner wanting to dissect the disagreement and examine each and every component, while the other wants to go off and mentally process the problem from a holistic perspective. This can create great frustration, with one partner wanting to resolve the issue and move on while the other is uncomfortable discussing deep feelings and thus creates emotional distance as a defense mechanism. Greater recognition of these style differences will provide the patience and understanding that are required to resolve conflicts when they arise. This couple could also benefit from greater exposure to the peacefulness and beauties of nature, and other physical activities that require no deep thinking or problem solving.

There is a key question you should ask yourself whenever a conflict arises in your relationship, "Would this issue matter if I were in the woods, or to a three-year old?" Your answer to this question will help you to ascertain whether or not the source of the conflict is arising from vital life sustaining aspects of your relationship or from a more distant place defined by social or ego pressures? If your answer is yes, recognize that the conflict has the power to destroy your relationship if not resolved satisfactorily. If your answer is no, there is a good chance the conflict may be less serious and may require an alternative approach to resolution.

E-Type Combination 1/6

Master   Closet Rebel

General Nature of Your Relationship

This couple can be characterized as survivors. Their relationship is based on the interaction between a partner who tends to find error and correct it and one who sees authority and doubts it. The bond in this relationship is based on hard work, self-sacrifice and the striving toward the achievement of cherished goals. There can be a negative tinge to this union, with one partner preoccupied with finding error and the other expressing doubt; however, there is an endurance quality that becomes established that can result in a deep sense of connection, admiration and respect. Prepared for adversity, this couple has the determination to overcome life's slings and arrows.

Primary Sources of Conflict

The primary source of conflict arises whenever the Master becomes critical and expresses dissatisfaction with the Closet Rebel for what appears to be slowness, caution and lack of direction. Often expressions of frustration arise such as, "Why can't you move faster?" "Stop dragging your feet," or, "Stop being so suspicious of everyone and everything." Masters feel that anger is wrong and Closet Rebels want to avoid it altogether, so conflicts can fester; one partner's effort feels like 'pushing on a string' while the other exhibits feelings of rebellion.

Recommended Courses of Action

This couple can benefit greatly from improved communications. One partner's critical nature needs to be countered by the other's sense of loyalty and commitment to shared ideals. Keeping lines of communication open will go a long way toward warding off annoying and destructive conflicts. Also, since disagreements tend to arise around performance issues, a clear understanding of mutual accountability needs to be established between the partners for tasks of an important nature.

There is a key question you should ask yourself whenever a conflict arises in your relationship, "Would this issue matter if I were in the woods, or to a three-year old?" Your answer to this question will help you to ascertain whether or not the source of the conflict is arising from vital life sustaining aspects of your relationship or from a more distant place defined by social or ego pressures? If your answer is yes, recognize that the conflict has the power to destroy your relationship if not resolved satisfactorily. If your answer is no, there is a good chance the conflict may be less serious and may require an alternative approach to resolution.

E-Type Combination 1/7

Master   Cruise Director

General Nature of Your Relationship

This relationship functions with one partner providing the stability and organization while the other provides the fun and excitement. Each partner is enhanced by the energy of the other. If this relationship were a dish, the Master would be the meat and potatoes while the Cruise Director would be the spice. One partner focuses on practicality while the other loves adventure and expansion into the unknown.

Primary Sources of Conflict

Conflicts can arise in this relationship when one partner appears one-dimensional and boring while the other is perceived to be illogical and impractical. In disagreements, the Master attempts to reign in the Cruise Director, which results in rebellion and the rejection of any form of imposed limits. One partner states, "That's not acceptable," while the other states, "You have a problem." Under stress the Master becomes inflexible, while the Cruise Director attempts to escape.

Recommended Courses of Action

This couple naturally interconnects by contributing highly desirable complementary aspects to the relationship. Points of conflict arise when one partner's need for structure and control conflicts with the other's need for spontaneity and freedom. This often results in comments such as, "You have no plan," which may receive a response like, "Stop trying to control me." Open discussions regarding differences, rather than vitriol and avoidance, will result in a much healthier relationship. The goal is to create balance between two dissimilar personalities that provide needed attributes to each other, one functioning as the anchor, the other the boat.

There is a key question you should ask yourself whenever a conflict arises in your relationship, "Would this issue matter if I were in the woods, or to a three-year old?" Your answer to this question will help you to ascertain whether or not the source of the conflict is arising from vital life sustaining aspects of your relationship or from a more distant place defined by social or ego pressures? If your answer is yes, recognize that the conflict has the power to destroy your relationship if not resolved satisfactorily. If your answer is no, there is a good chance the conflict may be less serious and may require an alternative approach to resolution.

E-Type Combination 1/8

Master   Conquistador

General Nature of Your Relationship

This is a highly combustible relationship where fireworks can occur at any moment. Masters struggle to be disciplined and correct while Conquistadors like to break the rules and roam free. Each has anger lurking beneath the surface of their personality. This couple has the potential for great success due to their combined nature of disciplined effort and strong desire to succeed. One partner secretly admires the daring and lack of restraint of their partner while the other respects the diligence and dedication exhibited by the other.

Primary Sources of Conflict

Conflict erupts in this relationship due to the volatile nature of the personalities involved. Neither spouse avoids confrontation when the issue of who is right is at stake. Both will fight tooth and nail to win an argument. Often things are said that are later regretted. Tensions rise when one partner presents a listing of unassailable facts while the other focuses on the underlying truth of the matter. Often the blowup clears the air and both parties move on with greater clarity. Seldom do these partners hold a grudge for long periods. "We fought. I won," is the typical conclusion of both parties.

Recommended Courses of Action

It is essential that both partners recognize the volatile nature and sheer energy that characterize this relationship.

Watching these two go at it may shock outside observers, but those in the family would say, "That is just how they are," or "It will be over in a minute." It would be helpful if this couple dialed back any personal attacks during these conflicts so no enduring damage is done to the relationship.

There is a key question you should ask yourself whenever a conflict arises in your relationship, "Would this issue matter if I were in the woods, or to a three-year old?" Your answer to this question will help you to ascertain whether or not the source of the conflict is arising from vital life sustaining aspects of your relationship or from a more distant place defined by social or ego pressures? If your answer is yes, recognize that the conflict has the power to destroy your relationship if not resolved satisfactorily. If your answer is no, there is a good chance the conflict may be less serious and may require an alternative approach to resolution.

E-Type Combination 1/9

Master   Harmonizer

General Nature of Your Relationship

This relationship can be characterized as generally amiable, with both partners desiring a peaceful and supportive home. While the Master provides the energy to pursue activities, the Harmonizer provides the support and stability for the partnership to achieve its objectives. Generally, one partner commits to a course of action and the other goes along and provides the support required to complete the mission. There is a reciprocal nature between these partners that is endearing and beneficial.

Primary Sources of Conflict

Conflict occurs in this relationship when an important decision needs to be made. The Master moves into action mode and drives toward a decision; the Harmonizer then stalls and retreats and has difficulty filtering out all of the alternatives. This results in exasperation and conflict. Both of these partners exhibit underlying anger with statements such as, "Be specific, tell me what you want!" and "Stop pushing me!" respectively. Masters focus on imperfections and blemishes and can become overcritical of their partners when under stress. Harmonizers are uncomfortable with conflict and oversensitive to criticism, resulting in hurt feelings and passive aggression, with inner thoughts such as, "You hurt me, now I won't give you what you want."

Recommended Courses of Action

This couple has the potential to coexist in a calm and mutually beneficial fashion. It is important for the Master to recognize that forcing a decision upon the Harmonizer is not a good strategy; rather than being impatient, it would be beneficial to provide information and the time required for the partner to get on board. Resistance does not always mean disagreement, only indecision. The Harmonizer needs to understand that the partner is trying to do the right thing and not make a mistake.

There is a key question you should ask yourself whenever a conflict arises in your relationship, "Would this issue matter if I were in the woods, or to a three-year old?" Your answer to this question will help you to ascertain whether or not the source of the conflict is arising from vital life sustaining aspects of your relationship or from a more distant place defined by social or ego pressures? If your answer is yes, recognize that the conflict has the power to destroy your relationship if not resolved satisfactorily. If your answer is no, there is a good chance the conflict may be less serious and may require an alternative approach to resolution.

E-Type Combination 2/2

Enchanter   Enchanter

General Nature of Your Relationship

Two Enchanters in a marriage create an interesting paradox. Both partners define themselves through the relationships they establish with others. The linkage is established through their helpfulness and giving nature. They connect with others by satisfying their needs for support and affection. This makes them indispensable, and is also the seat of their power and influence. However, this marriage may look like two people living separate lives.

Neither party is comfortable taking the lead and prefers to act in a support role rather than as a leader.

Primary Sources of Conflict

With little alpha energy existing in this relationship, much frustration is experienced while waiting for one or the other partner to take the lead. Even though great compassion exists between the partners, staleness or dreariness can set in. This is due to both partners being dependent upon the needs of the other to feel alive and experience joy. Both stand waiting to help the other, but no nucleus appears. Conflict erupts whenever one partner is required to become the center of attention and take the initiative.

Recommended Courses of Action

Enchanters are wonderful, supportive and compassionate people. The product of their lives is the love and attention they give to family and friends. Deep inside they are afraid of rejection, which is why they function as Enchanters: "If I help you, you won't reject me." Also, there is a quiet desperation for love in their lives: "If I shower you with love, you will love me back." It would be very beneficial for this couple to better understand the pillars of their personality and the veiled motivations behind their actions. You are not appendages of others, but possess a singular identity that needs to be strengthened and introduced to the world.

There is a key question you should ask yourself whenever a conflict arises in your relationship, "Would this issue matter if I were in the woods, or to a three-year old?" Your answer to this question will help you to ascertain whether or not the source of the conflict is arising from vital life sustaining aspects of your relationship or from a more distant place defined by social or ego pressures? If your answer is yes, recognize that the conflict has the power to destroy your relationship if not resolved satisfactorily. If your answer is no, there is a good chance the conflict may be less serious and may require an alternative approach to resolution.

E-Type Combination 2/3

Enchanter   Star

General Nature of Your Relationship

This relationship functions as two energy sources moving in the same direction. The Star tends to be actively involved and engaged in areas of interest while the Enchanter provides the stability and support the relationship requires. The theme of this combination is a striving for achievement and success, however that may be defined by the couple. The merging of these two personality types results in a special connection whereby each partner naturally provides for, and fulfills the needs of, the other without much effort or struggle.

Primary Sources of Conflict

If one looks at the needs of each partner, one requires winning while the other requires love and attention. When conflicts arise they are usually manifested by the Star being too focused on achievement or major areas of interest, and unwittingly ignoring the emotional needs of the partner.

Conversely, they may occur when one partner's goals are being thwarted and, out of frustration, that partner accuses the other of providing insufficient support. When the needs of both partners are being fulfilled this relationship is smooth sailing; however, when heartfelt desires become frustrated, flashpoints are likely to intervene in the relationship.

Recommended Courses of Action

The key to the health of this union is the achievement of balance. Both partners need to monitor their activities to ensure the Star does not overwork or over commit to the exclusion of the love and attention needed by the Enchanter. Alternatively, the Enchanter needs to remain vigilant and self aware to ensure the emotional support expected from the spouse is rational and appropriate.

There is a key question you should ask yourself whenever a conflict arises in your relationship, "Would this issue matter if I were in the woods, or to a three-year old?" Your answer to this question will help you to ascertain whether or not the source of the conflict is arising from vital life sustaining aspects of your relationship or from a more distant place defined by social or ego pressures? If your answer is yes, recognize that the conflict has the power to destroy your relationship if not resolved satisfactorily. If your answer is no, there is a good chance the conflict may be less serious and may require an alternative approach to resolution.

E-Type Combination 2/4

Enchanter   Drama Queen

General Nature of Your Relationship

This relationship can be characterized by its cat and mouse interaction. The Enchanter desires to maintain a strong and stable emotional connection while the Drama Queen is first inviting, then rejecting, thus offering a potpourri of erratic emotions. This can become a mutually supportive and loving relationship because the Enchanter needs someone to help and support while the Drama Queen needs and appreciates the help and attention. Also, there is more than a little charisma within this relationship and socially, this could be an interesting and stunning couple, with one partner offering the caring and warmth while the other adds allure and excitement.

Primary Sources of Conflict

Conflict occurs between this couple when all semblance of stability and predictability is lost. The Drama Queen can be emotionally mercurial, with wide swings in passionate expression, while the Enchanter needs the love and support offered by a more stable and reliable union. Any time there is tension both partners feel rejected and insecure, sending them back to one another with apologies and forgiveness: "We are afraid to be together, yet afraid to be apart."

Recommended Courses of Action

There is a temperamental nature to this relationship that needs to be managed and controlled so that it does not throw the relationship out of orbit. When conflict erupts, both partners suffer intensely. One partner has a fervent need for love and attention, while the other's primary need is for acknowledgement and acceptance. This couple should freely discuss their relationship on a regular basis, focusing on actions that both support and retard the health of the union. Increased sensitivity to the needs of each partner is the goal of this dialog.

There is a key question you should ask yourself whenever a conflict arises in your relationship, "Would this issue matter if I were in the woods, or to a three-year old?" Your answer to this question will help you to ascertain whether or not the source of the conflict is arising from vital life sustaining aspects of your relationship or from a more distant place defined by social or ego pressures? If your answer is yes, recognize that the conflict has the power to destroy your relationship if not resolved satisfactorily. If your answer is no, there is a good chance the conflict may be less serious and may require an alternative approach to resolution.

E-Type Combination 2/5

Enchanter　　　　　　　Solitary Mystic

General Nature of Your Relationship

This relationship may be characterized as the attraction of opposites. While one partner moves toward other people and is drawn to social interaction, the other partner withdraws and remains aloof from others. One partner functions from the feeling center, the other from the cognitive center. One partner reaches out, the other reaches in. One partner cares what other people think, the other does not. One is dependent while the other is independent. There is a 'push/pull' dynamic to this relationship, in which opposite energies both repel and attract, with both partners needing and valuing the attributes of the other.

Primary Sources of Conflict

The Enchanter in this relationship can feel lonely and abandoned upon occasion. The activities bringing the most joy to this partner have little interest for the other: "I don't want to go there. It's boring." The Solitary Mystic may also think the partner, operating from the feeling center, lacks depth and intellectual substance, thus creating feelings of separation and distance: "I can't talk to you about that, you wouldn't understand." These large disparities in needs and energy patterns can become a major source of conflict. "I need people," may receive a response of, "Then go alone."

Recommended Courses of Action

This couple, being opposites, have the opportunity to introduce complementary personality attributes into the relationship. The Solitary Mystic needs more feeling and connection with others while the Enchanter needs to be more analytical and introspective. The elements for growth are present within this relationship. This union is dependent upon compromise more than most: "I'll go to the party as long as I can leave by 9:00." It would be most beneficial if this couple established specific ground rules for their social activities. "I'll do that for you if you'll do this for me."

There is a key question you should ask yourself whenever a conflict arises in your relationship, "Would this issue matter if I were in the woods, or to a three-year old?" Your answer to this question will help you to ascertain whether or not the source of the conflict is arising from vital life sustaining aspects of your relationship or from a more distant place defined by social or ego pressures? If your answer is yes, recognize that the conflict has the power to destroy your relationship if not resolved satisfactorily. If your answer is no, there is a good chance the conflict may be less serious and may require an alternative approach to resolution.

E-Type Combination 2/6

Enchanter   Closet Rebel

General Nature of Your Relationship

This relationship may be characterized as one partner extending energy and support in order to overcome the other partner's reluctance to take risks and move forward. While one partner shows optimism, the other skepticism. There is an energizing quality to this relationship when it becomes committed to overcoming the odds or helping the underdog. Underneath, the Closet Rebel feels like 'shoving it to the man' and shows suspicion of others' motives. When these qualities become coupled with the love and affection naturally supplied by the Enchanter, the basis of a more positive and productive symmetry is established within the relationship.

Primary Sources of Conflict

Conflict can arise in this relationship when one partner is more desirous of getting ahead in life than the other. The Enchanter may 'want more' and press the Closet Rebel into making necessary changes only to be greeted by resistance, reluctance and suspicion: "Aren't I good enough for you?" Given this response, the Enchanter may become critical of the partner's level of effort and unwillingness to show more initiative. Also, the Enchanter may become exhausted trying to overcome the overall suspicion and skepticism at the core of the Closet Rebel's personality. "What are you afraid of?" In addition, the Closet Rebel may be more than a bit suspicious of the Enchanter's urging for more progress in life: "Stop nagging!"

Recommended Courses of Action

A bond of trust and a 'you and me against the world' connection needs to exist at the center of this relationship. Rather than operating as two coexisting individuals, it needs to be viewed and operate as one functioning entity. Any actions that help the Closet Rebel feel more safe and secure and the Enchanter more loved and appreciated will be successful.

There is a key question you should ask yourself whenever a conflict arises in your relationship, "Would this issue matter if I were in the woods, or to a three-year old?" Your answer to this question will help you to ascertain whether or not the source of the conflict is arising from vital life sustaining aspects of your relationship or from a more

distant place defined by social or ego pressures? If your answer is yes, recognize that the conflict has the power to destroy your relationship if not resolved satisfactorily. If your answer is no, there is a good chance the conflict may be less serious and may require an alternative approach to resolution.

E-Type Combination 2/7

Enchanter   Cruise Director

General Nature of Your Relationship

This couple exudes a magnetic attraction that draws other people into their orbit. The Cruise Director establishes the direction while the Enchanter provides the necessary support. Usually there is excitement swirling around this couple, with people coming and going and interesting events underway or being planned. The Enchanter helps the partner to focus while the Cruise Director provides the excitement and adventure. The mutuality of their interaction tends to provide the security and stability needed to prevent this relationship from spinning out of control.

Primary Sources of Conflict

The Cruise Director rejects anything that limits her desire for a broad range of potential experiences. Enchanters react whenever they feel ignored or not included in their partners' activities. While one partner can easily function independently, the other partner is more dependent upon the plans, activities and direction offered by the other: "Tell me what you want to do and we'll do it together." Under the worst of conditions, the Cruise Director may see the Enchanter as overly dependent and a drag on their activities, while the Enchanter may view the Cruise Director as superficial and lacking depth. Therefore, conflict occurs when one partner's course and trajectory do not sufficiently integrate the other's needs and desires.

Recommended Courses of Action

This is an appealing couple capable of living an interesting and pleasant life together. While one partner requires freedom of action, the other needs to feel loved and appreciated. The Enchanter must provide the partner with a modicum of restraint; the Cruise Director must ensure that the partner is never left behind when planning life events. One partner needs to prevent the relationship from slipping into self-indulgence while the other needs to avert it from becoming consumed by emotion and dependency.

There is a key question you should ask yourself whenever a conflict arises in your relationship, "Would this issue matter if I were in the woods, or to a three-year old?" Your answer to this question will help you to ascertain whether or not the source of the conflict is arising from vital life sustaining aspects of your relationship or from a more distant place defined by social or ego pressures? If your answer is yes, recognize that the conflict has the power to destroy your relationship if not resolved satisfactorily. If your answer is no, there is a good chance the conflict may be less serious and may require an alternative approach to resolution.

E-Type Combination 2/8

Enchanter   Conquistador

General Nature of Your Relationship

This relationship may be characterized by one partner's dominant personality being matched with an accommodating partner. The Conquistador sets the agenda and the Enchanter gets into alignment with the force and energy of the partner. It is a union with much to offer both parties given that the energies are complementary, rather than opposed. The Conquistador needs to receive attention and the Enchanter needs to give it, therefore there is balance.

Primary Sources of Conflict

The risk of conflict arises in this relationship whenever the Enchanter attempts to set the agenda or place specific needs ahead of the partner's. This often results in a conflict of wills primarily because the Conquistador is accustomed to having his or her needs treated as a priority. There is a self-centeredness embedded within the Conquistador's personality that can create volatility when expressed in this relationship. The Enchanter, rather than directly challenging the partner, uses charm and attention to sway the outcome. Under stress this may be seen as an attempt at manipulation. One partner states, "I want to do it my way," while the other says, "I want your consideration."

Recommended Courses of Action

Under normal circumstances, this is a highly complementary relationship with both partners mutually fulfilling the needs of the other simply by expressing the intrinsic nature of their personalities. The Conquistador, by becoming a bit more accommodating, can help this relationship. The greater the sense of security felt by both partners, the smoother this relationship will function.

There is a key question you should ask yourself whenever a conflict arises in your relationship, "Would this issue matter if I were in the woods, or to a three-year old?" Your answer to this question will help you to ascertain whether or not the source of the conflict is arising from vital life sustaining aspects of your relationship or from a more distant place defined by social or ego pressures? If your answer is yes, recognize that the conflict has the power to destroy your relationship if not resolved satisfactorily. If your answer is no, there is a good chance the conflict may

be less serious and may require an alternative approach to resolution.

E-Type Combination 2/9

Enchanter   Harmonizer

General Nature of Your Relationship

This couple appears to be very similar in nature, reaching out to others in a helpful and affectionate manner. Both have the capacity to adapt their personalities to the needs of others; in fact, they are more comfortable doing so than focusing on their own individual requirements. This relationship can be characterized as 'other-centric' and both members possess the innate capacity to satisfy the needs of their partners. The Enchanter is happiest when helping the partner fulfill his or her deepest potential, while the Harmonizer desires to merge with the mate. There is a reciprocal energy in this relationship with love and tenderness at its center.

Primary Sources of Conflict

There is a deep-seated dependency built into this relationship. Both partners define their identity through the bond they share with one another. If anything intervenes to threaten this bond both partners react vigorously, causing tension and conflict. Feelings of jealousy, anger and betrayal may erupt. The Enchanter wants the Harmonizer to achieve full potential while the Harmonizer wants the partner to be totally authentic. When either of these goals is not achieved, conflict will develop over time.

Recommended Courses of Action

Harmonizers need to be jump-started and Enchanters supply the spark. This relationship works best whenever there are shared goals and unity of action. It is very important that this couple aligns their energies toward commonly agreed-upon targets, rather than individual aspirations. Specific goals and direction need to be instituted, rather than passive acceptance of the status quo.

There is a key question you should ask yourself whenever a conflict arises in your relationship, "Would this issue matter if I were in the woods, or to a three-year old?" Your answer to this question will help you to ascertain whether or not the source of the conflict is arising from vital life sustaining aspects of your relationship or from a more distant place defined by social or ego pressures? If your answer is yes, recognize that the conflict has the power to destroy your relationship if not resolved satisfactorily. If your answer is no, there is a good chance the conflict may be less serious and may require an alternative approach to resolution.

E-Type Combination 3/3

Star   Star

General Nature of Your Relationship

This relationship can be described by the following words: busy, intense, image, winning and social. Two Stars in a relationship have no restraining influences on their ambition. This liaison can appear perfect on the outside and be troubled on the inside because of the intense striving and the unrestrained need to achieve. This union succeeds whenever both partners triumph in different arenas and do not become competitive with one another.

Primary Sources of Conflict

Given the nature of a two Star couple, the image of a gerbil running on a wheel comes to mind. There comes a point when the questions, "Are we going anywhere important?" and "What's the point of all of this activity?" must be asked. Conflict may arise if one partner decides to become more introspective and go for a more meaningful life when the other does not want to stop and smell the roses. By their nature, Stars find it difficult to delve inside to find meaningful and lasting answers. They much prefer functioning from the surface of their personalities.

Recommended Courses of Action

This couple needs to turn inward to add more meaning to their lives. An inventory of all aspects of their lives should be taken, and anything considered superficial should be discarded. A deeper and more authentic emotional bond is the order of the day. This will be a challenge for both partners because at first, it will feel unnatural. However it represents the best path forward to greater happiness and peace.

There is a key question you should ask yourself whenever a conflict arises in your relationship, "Would this issue matter if I were in the woods, or to a three-year old?" Your answer to this question will help you to ascertain whether or not the source of the conflict is arising from vital life sustaining aspects of your relationship or from a more distant place defined by social or ego pressures? If your answer is yes, recognize that the conflict has the power to destroy your relationship if not resolved satisfactorily. If your answer is no, there is a good chance the conflict may be less serious and may require an alternative approach to resolution.

E-Type Combination 3/4

Star   Drama Queen

General Nature of Your Relationship

This couple may be characterized as stylish and elegant. One partner brings the dedication and competitiveness while the other brings the artistry and emotion. Under good conditions this is a knockout pairing since both partners are focused on public appearance and the respect they receive from other people. This couple has divergent needs, with the Star requiring success and the Drama Queen emotional intimacy. One partner appears preoccupied while the other strives to break through and connect on a deeper emotional level.

Primary Sources of Conflict

The primary source of conflict for this pairing has to do with one partner's focus on the outside world while the other longs for personal intimacy: "Don't you dare call your broker! This is our anniversary dinner." When the Star becomes preoccupied with outside activities and loses connection with the Drama Queen, conflicts arise: "I need your attention. Why don't you ever listen to me?" "I know, I know. I'll do better in the future." By nature, Stars are not highly emotional, while Drama Queens feed on emotion.

Recommended Courses of Action

It is unlikely that a Star will ever completely understand the longing, tumultuous and sensitive nature of the Drama Queen. The best approach for the Star is to transcend the specifics of the relationship with the following theme: "I will love you until the end of time no matter what. Everything else in our life is a footnote. Everything I do, I do for us." The Drama Queen needs to understand the fundamental cause of the emotional breaches that may occur from time to time and help the Star take baby steps in the direction of greater intimacy.

There is a key question you should ask yourself whenever a conflict arises in your relationship, "Would this issue matter if I were in the woods, or to a three-year old?" Your answer to this question will help you to ascertain whether or not the source of the conflict is arising from vital life sustaining aspects of your relationship or from a more distant place defined by social or ego pressures? If your answer is yes, recognize that the conflict has the power to destroy your relationship if not resolved satisfactorily. If your answer is no, there is a good chance the conflict may be less serious and may require an alternative approach to resolution.

E-Type Combination 3/5

Star   Solitary Mystic

General Nature of Your Relationship

Two partners operating in parallel but separate orbits may characterize this relationship. Each has the capacity for extraordinary achievement, but usually in completely different venues. While the Star usually functions as a model performer, highly social and outgoing, the Solitary Mystic achieves through more introverted and mental pursuits. "I run a business," as opposed to, "I'm a senior software engineer." This relationship works because neither partner needs a great deal of emotional support. When this couple interacts it resembles a lunar eclipse, everything goes dark and then light appears – a momentary interlude. "Let's meet for lunch." "Ok. Where do you want to go?"

Primary Sources of Conflict

There are two primary sources of conflict built into this relationship. First, The Star thrives on social contact and needs to be socially active to feel in sync; the Solitary

Mystic is reclusive by nature and finds socializing to be either boring or draining. This is a structural conflict caused by the intrinsic yet conflicting nature of both partners. The second area of potential conflict occurs when the Star becomes overly committed to outside activities and the Solitary Mystic wants to rein the partner in. One partner feels restricted while the other insecure.

Recommended Courses of Action

The energies within this relationship are complementary, not adversarial. These partners will benefit from the establishment of specific ground rules for their activities: "How much time will this take?" "Would three hours be too much?" When Solitary Mystics know what to expect, it removes the potential for social anxiety to arise from shared activities. This partner feels as though it is a sacrifice to give up private time, while the Star is energized by social engagement.

There is a key question you should ask yourself whenever a conflict arises in your relationship, "Would this issue matter if I were in the woods, or to a three-year old?" Your answer to this question will help you to ascertain whether or not the source of the conflict is arising from vital life sustaining aspects of your relationship or from a more distant place defined by social or ego pressures? If your answer is yes, recognize that the conflict has the power to destroy your relationship if not resolved satisfactorily. If your answer is no, there is a good chance the conflict may be less serious and may require an alternative approach to resolution.

E-Type Combination 3/6

Star   Closet Rebel

General Nature of Your Relationship

This relationship has divergent energies integrated within it. While the Star desires to meet the world confidently and assertively, the Closet Rebel is more hesitant and doubtful. While one partner enjoys being the center of attention, the other is suspicious of it. While one partner is progressive, the other is regressive. Under optimum circumstances the Star helps the Closet Rebel by encouraging greater self-confidence and trust, while the Closet Rebel helps the Star become more authentic and aware of deeper emotions.

Primary Sources of Conflict

Conflict arises in this relationship from the sheer differences in perspective held by the partners. The purposeful resistance and doubtfulness of the partner can frustrate the Star, while the Closet Rebel can resent and be suspicious of the partner's work ethic and success: "Stop being so negative all the time," versus, "All you do is work. This could all end tomorrow." While the Star sees the future in terms of how great it could be, the Closet Rebel invokes all the obstacles and problems that could be encountered along the way. "You're a drag." "You're a dreamer."

Recommended Courses of Action

Recognition and accomplishment should not be the only measure of success for this union. Success without meaning feels empty. The Star needs to help the Closet Rebel to overcome the doubt and suspicion that can suppress the joy experienced from the relationship; the Closet Rebel needs to help the Star understand there is more to life than self-promotion and winning. Acknowledging and talking through the differences that exist within this relationship will go a long way toward strengthening this union.

There is a key question you should ask yourself whenever a conflict arises in your relationship, "Would this issue matter if I were in the woods, or to a three-year old?" Your answer to this question will help you to ascertain whether or not the source of the conflict is arising from vital life sustaining aspects of your relationship or from a more distant place defined by social or ego pressures? If your answer is yes, recognize that the conflict has the power to destroy your relationship if not resolved satisfactorily. If your answer is no, there is a good chance the conflict may be less serious and may require an alternative approach to resolution.

E-Type Combination 3/7

Star   Cruise Director

General Nature of Your Relationship

This is a well-matched family unit full of fun, adventure and opportunity. It is best described as a relationship in motion. Both partners move through life in a positive fashion and draw others along with them. "What would you like to do for your birthday? I know. Let's have a party and invite the whole neighborhood." At times there does not seem to be a governor on this engine and it is very easy for these partners to become overextended. All in all, this is a 'most likely to succeed' pairing.

Primary Sources of Conflict

The best image for this couple is a spinning top, whirling and whirling until gravity prevails. Gravity, in this case, is the harshness of reality. This couple can be moving in so many different directions that it is not until life intervenes that they stop and analyze present circumstances. Conflicts occur in this relationship not due to incompatibilities, but due to overextension. This is not a couple that spends much time analyzing day-to-day issues. Conflict arises when reality asserts itself. "How could this have happened?" "I don't know. It just came out of nowhere." The pleasant parts of this relationship can be overemphasized and the deficiencies overlooked or ignored.

Recommended Courses of Action

This couple can deceive itself that everything is fine when its not. The Star feels most secure when fully engaged in outside activities while the Cruise Director projects exciting plans and activities into the future. Both of these can become avoidant behaviors. "We don't like to dwell on the negative." Ensuring that time is set aside each week to do something relaxing and intimate together, and working through anxieties and troubles when they arise, can best serve this couple.

There is a key question you should ask yourself whenever a conflict arises in your relationship, "Would this issue matter if I were in the woods, or to a three-year old?" Your answer to this question will help you to ascertain whether or not the source of the conflict is arising from vital life sustaining aspects of your relationship or from a more distant place defined by social or ego pressures? If your answer is yes, recognize that the conflict has the power to destroy your relationship if not resolved satisfactorily. If your answer is no, there is a good chance the conflict may be less serious and may require an alternative approach to resolution.

E-Type Combination 3/8

Star   Conquistador

General Nature of Your Relationship

This relationship can be described by the Shakespearean term 'star-crossed lovers', meaning not favored by the stars. Both of these partners are accustomed to getting their own way. Both are dominant and powerful personalities and feel anxiety when expressing deeply held emotions. The Star wants to win through image and persuasion while the Conquistador wants to conquer through the use of force, even though the behavior is wrapped in platitudes. Both of these partners are willing to expend large amounts of energy to get what they want. As a family unit this union could be described as tumultuous.

Primary Sources of Conflict

Conflict arises in this relationship from the expression of the intrinsic nature of the respective personalities. This conflict may be described as structural in nature. Both partners insist on being the dominant and controlling force within the relationship. It is inconceivable to them that they would play a subservient role in a partnership; therefore, conflict is an integral aspect of this combination. When one partner prevails over the other, the compliant partner feels diminished and weakened, which becomes an intolerable emotion except for very short intervals. There is an unspoken message in this relationship, "Look, we both know that I am stronger (smarter) than you so let's just do it my way." This is perceived as unfair, cruel and heartless, thus resulting in anger and conflict.

Recommended Courses of Action

This relationship could be improved by operating as a business partnership; both partners are owners who share the pain as well as the rewards equally. A niche should be carved out so that each individual makes unique and specific contributions to the enterprise based on interests and aptitudes. Both parties must be willing to make compromises for this union to be successful.

There is a key question you should ask yourself whenever a conflict arises in your relationship, "Would this issue matter if I were in the woods, or to a three-year old?" Your answer to this question will help you to ascertain whether or not the source of the conflict is arising from vital life sustaining aspects of your relationship or from a more

distant place defined by social or ego pressures? If your answer is yes, recognize that the conflict has the power to destroy your relationship if not resolved satisfactorily. If your answer is no, there is a good chance the conflict may be less serious and may require an alternative approach to resolution.

E-Type Combination 3/9

Star   Harmonizer

General Nature of Your Relationship

This is a compatible union, with one partner establishing the direction of the relationship while the other adopts and supports mutual goals. The Star is the action-oriented partner, while the Harmonizer enables the Star to reach full potential. This can be a highly productive combination, particularly whenever there is a merging of deep inner goals by both parties. The Harmonizer feels secure whenever focusing on a path that the partner spearheaded. "I didn't really know what I wanted until I met you." Because the Harmonizer is so adept at fulfilling the goals of the partner, the Star becomes unleashed and more focused on outside activities without being drained by diversions adeptly handled by the partner.

Primary Sources of Conflict

Conflict arises in this union whenever there is a breach in the relationship caused by the Star being distanced from the partner, primarily by life circumstances. This becomes threatening to the Harmonizer because identity and feelings of security are dependent upon their partner's energy and direction. Harmonizers have a very difficult time with self-definition and find it much easier to simply accept their partner's persona as their own. Another source of conflict arises whenever the Harmonizer attempts to engage the partner in a discussion that may involve painful emotions. "Do we really need to talk about that right now?"

Recommended Courses of Action

Both partners can benefit from self-identity work. Stars have a chameleon-like quality, they can quickly become whatever the circumstances call for and this raises authenticity issues; the Harmonizer has not sufficiently self-differentiated. Both partners need to explore these areas of self-development. Progress will yield significant benefits to this relationship.

There is a key question you should ask yourself whenever a conflict arises in your relationship, "Would this issue matter if I were in the woods, or to a three-year old?" Your answer to this question will help you to ascertain whether or not the source of the conflict is arising from vital life sustaining aspects of your relationship or from a more distant place defined by social or ego pressures? If your answer is yes, recognize that the conflict has the power to destroy your relationship if not resolved satisfactorily. If your answer is no, there is a good chance the conflict may be less serious and may require an alternative approach to resolution.

E-Type Combination 4/4

Drama Queen   Drama Queen

General Nature of Your Relationship

This couple's relationship is straight out of a Russian novel, full of pathos, lusty sex, glamour and loss. Often this union is formed later in life and is based on the recognition of common interests and similarities existing between this couple. "I never thought anyone could feel as intensely as I do until I met you." This can be a raucous relationship, with wild swings between despondency and elation. Fights arise and then blow over. The air is cleared and the couple moves on. The undercurrent of this partnership is instability couched in passion.

Primary Sources of Conflict

Both members of this partnership are in search of an intense and all-encompassing love connection, a metaphysical bonding of sorts, that transcends the bounds of the ordinary. "I don't want you to love me, I want you to merge with me." The peak experiences that arise momentarily are fleeting, and therefore the relationship can be perceived as lacking some essential element. This can result in a barrage of criticism and dissatisfaction directed at the offending partner which is magnified by both partners' search for the same transcendent connection. "If you were right for me I wouldn't feel so down all the time." "All you do is criticize."

Recommended Courses of Action

It should be recognized that this couple is looking for love in all the wrong places. The overwhelming desire for an intense love connection is an attempt to replace negative subconscious feelings of being deeply flawed and inadequate. The primary way to improve this relationship is to recognize that it is unreasonable for you to expect another person to remove your feelings of despair; only you have that power. By resolving your own subconscious conflicts, you, in turn, improve the overall satisfaction with your relationship.

There is a key question you should ask yourself whenever a conflict arises in your relationship, "Would this issue matter if I were in the woods, or to a three-year old?" Your answer to this question will help you to ascertain whether or not the source of the conflict is arising from vital life sustaining aspects of your relationship or from a more

distant place defined by social or ego pressures? If your answer is yes, recognize that the conflict has the power to destroy your relationship if not resolved satisfactorily. If your answer is no, there is a good chance the conflict may be less serious and may require an alternative approach to resolution.

E-Type Combination 4/5

Drama Queen   Solitary Mystic

General Nature of Your Relationship

Two different perceptual channels dominate this relationship: the heart and the mind. One partner interprets the world through feelings, the other through mental processing. One is expansive emotionally, the other is emotionally regressive. Surprisingly, both partners can be enriched in this pairing through the attraction of opposites. "You delight me with your knowledge." "You enthrall me with your style." Successful couplings tend to evolve over time, whereby the Drama Queen draws her partner out emotionally while the Solitary Mystic lessens his partner's overt need for attention. This results in a nicely balanced and functional family unit.

Primary Sources of Conflict

Conflict occurs in this relationship when the expressed needs of the Drama Queen are interpreted as being excessive and the Solitary Mystic withdraws. Drama Queens react strongly when they perceive a lack of attention, while the Solitary Mystic withdraws when feeling intense emotion. This can create a serious rift in this relationship because the reactions of both partners are spawned deep within their psyches. One is moving forward to attain while the other is moving back to avoid. "You don't spend enough time with me." "You require too much of me."

Recommended Courses of Action

These partners possess acute levels of sensitivity and awareness. These attributes may be utilized to improve the overall quality of this pairing. The shared appreciation of a concert, movie, book, theatre, photo or art is quite high. Opportunities for such experiences should be pursued as much as possible. Usually the 'attraction quotient' between these individuals is quite high. It is essential that a balance be established whereby this couple makes it a priority to do interesting things together. If this is not accomplished it could result in two individuals essentially leading separate lives under one roof.

There is a key question you should ask yourself whenever a conflict arises in your relationship, "Would this issue matter if I were in the woods, or to a three-year old?" Your answer to this question will help you to ascertain whether or not the source of the conflict is arising from vital life sustaining aspects of your relationship or from a more distant place defined by social or ego pressures? If your answer is yes, recognize that the conflict has the power to destroy your relationship if not resolved satisfactorily. If your answer is no, there is a good chance the conflict may be less serious and may require an alternative approach to resolution.

E-Type Combination 4/6

Drama Queen   Closet Rebel

General Nature of Your Relationship

The binding element of this relationship is a general sense of being disconnected from the world. The Drama Queen experiences underlying fears of separation and abandonment while the Closet Rebel endures feelings of being misplaced or out of sync with society in general. This shared suffering tends to make this union stronger by creating an overall commitment to make things better. "Because things are hard doesn't mean we can't succeed." There is a transcendent quality of mutual support that is based on the confidence that "We can overcome the odds which have always been against us."

Primary Sources of Conflict

Conflicts can arise when one or both partners struggle to cope with their negative feelings. The Drama Queen secretly wants the partner to take responsibility for removing deeply rooted sorrowful feelings, while the Closet Rebel can be riddled with self-doubt. While one partner moves into hypercritical mode: "If you were right for me I wouldn't feel so sad all the time." The other becomes angry by a perceived lack of support: "If you really loved me you wouldn't kick me while I'm down.".

Recommended Courses of Action

This couple can benefit from establishing some ground rules for managing disagreements. Without these guidelines, anger can spill over and leap the bounds of restraint, which can cause long lasting damage to the relationship. The couple should never lose sight of the enduring quality that sustains this relationship. "We are in this together, forever." It would also be helpful if both partners realized the broad range of emotions being released into this relationship. One partner expresses feelings somewhere between joy and sadness, while the other experiences feelings ranging between confidence and doubt. Increased sensitivity to these swings of emotion can help provide greater balance to this union.

There is a key question you should ask yourself whenever a conflict arises in your relationship, "Would this issue matter if I were in the woods, or to a three-year old?" Your answer to this question will help you to ascertain whether or not the source of the conflict is arising from vital life

sustaining aspects of your relationship or from a more distant place defined by social or ego pressures? If your answer is yes, recognize that the conflict has the power to destroy your relationship if not resolved satisfactorily. If your answer is no, there is a good chance the conflict may be less serious and may require an alternative approach to resolution.

E-Type Combination 4/7

Drama Queen   Cruise Director

General Nature of Your Relationship

This relationship can be characterized as one partner focused on the acquisition of diverse activities while the other strives toward emotional connection. One partner is mind-centered and the other heart-centered. The union is successful when the Cruise Director leads the charge for varied and interesting activities, thus mitigating the periodic despondency felt by the Drama Queen. There is much to share between these partners, with the Cruise Director projecting innate optimism and a sense of excitement while the Drama Queen opens the way toward greater emotional depth and artistic sensibility.

Primary Sources of Conflict

The pairing of these two personality types is not always complementary because of the large differences between them. When these differences collide, conflicts can be created. The Cruise Director desires action and adventure and wants to avoid negativity as much as possible, while the Drama Queen plows a deep emotional furrow and wants passionate and intense conversations whenever problems arise. This can lead to an impasse, with one partner fleeing while the other falls into depression. "You never want to talk about problems in our relationship." "You never want to talk about anything but problems in our relationship."

Recommended Courses of Action

This couple needs to take measures to avoid the extremes of their personality types. The Cruise Director needs to acknowledge the Drama Queen's need for soul-to-soul conflict resolution, while the Drama Queen must ensure that irrational emotional longing and excessive neediness are not injected into the partnership. While one partner brings optimism to the relationship the other brings style and sensitivity. This is a winning combination when recognized and appreciated by both partners.

There is a key question you should ask yourself whenever a conflict arises in your relationship, "Would this issue matter if I were in the woods, or to a three-year old?" Your answer to this question will help you to ascertain whether or not the source of the conflict is arising from vital life sustaining aspects of your relationship or from a more distant place defined by social or ego pressures? If your answer is yes, recognize that the conflict has the power to destroy your relationship if not resolved satisfactorily. If your answer is no, there is a good chance the conflict may be less serious and may require an alternative approach to resolution.

E-Type Combination 4/8

Drama Queen   Conquistador

General Nature of Your Relationship

This relationship can be characterized as one of intense emotion, such as loud fights, lusty makeups, bold actions and demure enticements. It seems as though there is never a dull minute between these partners. While one partner is drawn to the style and refinement offered by one spouse, the other is attracted to the strength and sheer boldness of the other. This couple enjoys compensating attributes. While one partner needs the security and reliability of a dominant partner, the other needs the sensitivity and deeply felt support offered by the other. One partner values the truth above all; the other requires authentic emotional connection. "When we fight I discover the truth." "When we make up I feel the connection."

Primary Sources of Conflict

Conquistadors are notorious for their lack of restraint. They will violate the rules just to see if they can get away with it.

They can be insensitive, self-centered, itinerant and combative. You can imagine the conflict that may arise when these traits are coupled with a partner who is sensitive, demure, artistic, moody and requiring more than a little emotional maintenance. Tension in this relationship is likely to arise whenever the Conquistador moves into independent orbit and the Drama Queen feels left behind or diminished in some fashion. "I need more freedom." "I need to be with you more often."

Recommended Courses of Action

This is a complementary relationship, with one partner appreciating the style and refinement made available through the relationship, while the other admires the possibilities for assertiveness and bold direction. Both partners are enhanced by the availability of these attributes within the union. It will benefit this couple if one partner avoids becoming brutish and the other overly needy. Make it a priority to support each other's projects and initiatives, and never veer too far away from one another.

There is a key question you should ask yourself whenever a conflict arises in your relationship, "Would this issue matter if I were in the woods, or to a three-year old?" Your answer to this question will help you to ascertain whether or not the source of the conflict is arising from vital life

sustaining aspects of your relationship or from a more distant place defined by social or ego pressures? If your answer is yes, recognize that the conflict has the power to destroy your relationship if not resolved satisfactorily. If your answer is no, there is a good chance the conflict may be less serious and may require an alternative approach to resolution.

E-Type Combination 4/9

Drama Queen   Harmonizer

General Nature of Your Relationship

This statement may characterize this relationship; "I find it easy to love." These partners tend to adhere to one another through their emotional bonding. One partner is dedicated to maintaining an intense and deep emotional commitment while the other is happy to oblige. There are few roadblocks within this relationship, provided the Drama Queen does not become overly possessive and the Harmonizer stays connected and does not zone out. The nature of one partner is broadly accepting while the other vibrant and mercurial. The combination is magic in that both partners provide the most essential elements for a strong and robust relationship.

Primary Sources of Conflict

Conflicts arise when these partners emphasize the core negative aspects of their personalities: one partner wants more while the other appears emotionally absent. "I need more from you." "I'm doing the best I can." "You're flawed." "You're unrealistic." When the Harmonizer is perceived as not meeting the emotional needs of the Drama Queen, insults begin to fly and criticisms are advanced. The Harmonizer, lacking alternatives, creates distance from the partner, spending more time away, pursuing private interests.

Recommended Courses of Action

The Harmonizer wants to avoid conflict at all costs, while the Drama Queen wants to engage and process through conflicts in a deeply emotional way. This can raise the anxiety in the partner who doesn't feel capable of repairing the breach. "We've been through this before and nothing's changed." In conflict, the Harmonizer just stops doing anything and the Drama Queen becomes furious over the perceived neglect. It would be very beneficial for both parties to realize that each is acting out of type and not in purposeful antagonism. "We both have needs. Let's get this fixed."

There is a key question you should ask yourself whenever a conflict arises in your relationship, "Would this issue matter if I were in the woods, or to a three-year old?" Your answer to this question will help you to ascertain whether or not the source of the conflict is arising from vital life sustaining aspects of your relationship or from a more distant place defined by social or ego pressures? If your answer is yes, recognize that the conflict has the power to destroy your relationship if not resolved satisfactorily. If your answer is no, there is a good chance the conflict may be less serious and may require an alternative approach to resolution.

E-Type Combination 5/5

Solitary Mystic   Solitary Mystic

General Nature of Your Relationship

Two independent thinkers who require little social interaction living under one roof may characterize this relationship. Both partners need their own space and sufficient solitude to pursue their projects without interruption. Rooms may actually be allocated as 'his' and 'hers' to permit sufficient life space. Even though this couple can function independently, each needs the affection and support provided by the other to remain in equilibrium. "Let's meet at noon and go for a walk." "Ok. But I can only be gone for an hour." Because this couple does not create undue pressure on one another to socialize or become outwardly focused, it can provide both partners with a great deal of compatibility and satisfaction. Because the heart of this relationship is primarily mental, this couple can experience a strong love connection that is primarily nonverbal.

Primary Sources of Conflict

Under stress both partners possess the same instinct: to withdraw. This can become a major problem when one partner is moving toward the other to resolve a conflict and the other psychologically exits the relationship. Feelings of psychological abandonment often result. Because the Solitary Mystic tends to retreat emotionally from conflict, both partners may simply try to ignore or subvert negative emotions, which leaves them unresolved. This can become a very painful experience and can lead to intense suffering by both marriage partners. It is not until both partners fully process the conflict in all of its dimensions that resolution is possible.

Recommended Courses of Action

It would be beneficial for both partners to work on becoming more comfortable expressing their emotions without fear of being exposed or invaded in some way. This would enable resolution to occur without an extended period of withdrawal and pain. In addition, it would be beneficial if this couple became involved in an outside cause or project that would release them from their social isolation and enable them to share their knowledge and foresight with others.

There is a key question you should ask yourself whenever a conflict arises in your relationship, "Would this issue matter if I were in the woods, or to a three-year old?" Your answer to this question will help you to ascertain whether or not the source of the conflict is arising from vital life sustaining aspects of your relationship or from a more distant place defined by social or ego pressures? If your answer is yes, recognize that the conflict has the power to destroy your relationship if not resolved satisfactorily. If your answer is no, there is a good chance the conflict may be less serious and may require an alternative approach to resolution.

E-Type Combination 5/6

Solitary Mystic   Closet Rebel

General Nature of Your Relationship

This relationship may be characterized by quiet companionship, with both partners enjoying the peaceful coexistence that this union offers. While the Solitary Mystic requires independence and solitude, the Closet Rebel is more than happy to provide the initiative that keeps this couple relevant and moving forward. Neither partner places unrealistic demands upon the other; therefore conflicts may be something of a rarity. It may appear that some 'juice' is missing in this relationship due to its few outward signs of affection or sentimental offerings on display. Since this love connection is primarily mental, it may be that there is more affection and positive feeling exchanged between the couple than is evident to the casual observer.

Primary Sources of Conflict

Conflict in this relationship usually occurs when the Closet Rebel feels inadequate or threatened and moves toward the Solitary Mystic for reassurance. The Solitary Mystic, being emotionally withdrawn by nature, pulls away, thus reinforcing the partner's worst fears, which triggers a potentially paranoid overreaction. "I never believed you really loved me." "Why do I always feel you are withholding something from me?" Emotions are threatening to the Solitary Mystic, and therefore avoidance behavior becomes interpreted as lack of caring.

Recommended Courses of Action

The combination of these two distinctive personalities offers the potential for happiness and joy, provided sufficient insight into the needs and motivations of both partners exists within the relationship. The Solitary Mystic must guard against excessive detachment, while the Closet Rebel needs to have greater confidence in the durability of the relationship. Keeping the lines of communication open in this relationship is the key to overcoming obstacles.

There is a key question you should ask yourself whenever a conflict arises in your relationship, "Would this issue matter if I were in the woods, or to a three-year old?" Your answer to this question will help you to ascertain whether or not the source of the conflict is arising from vital life sustaining aspects of your relationship or from a more distant place defined by social or ego pressures? If your answer is yes, recognize that the conflict has the power to destroy your relationship if not resolved satisfactorily. If your answer is no, there is a good chance the conflict may be less serious and may require an alternative approach to resolution.

E-Type Combination 5/7

Solitary Mystic   Cruise Director

General Nature of Your Relationship

There are complementary energies within this relationship, with one partner supplying the fun and excitement while the other provides the bedrock substance. It may be characterized as a mutual need relationship in that the Cruise Director requires an anchor to prevent overextension while the Solitary Mystic needs a partner to stimulate social activity. When these two aspects are in balance, there is great chemistry within this union. Both partners value and are granted independence, and thus their basic natures are not thwarted by an overly restrictive partner.

Primary Sources of Conflict

This relationship can spin out of balance under two conditions: 1) the Cruise Director expends so much time and energy out of the house pursuing social activities that contact with the spouse is lost; 2) The Solitary Mystic becomes detached and preoccupied to such an extent that the relationship becomes zombified. Under both conditions the partners feel abandoned, disconnected and unloved. This usually results in a spillover of anger, which is actually disguised anxiety.

Recommended Courses of Action

It is very easy for these partners to become so engrossed in their independent activities that a spouse may accidentally be ignored or discounted in some fashion. This couple does not need a great deal of interaction to be happy; however, sufficient exchange of information will result in a greater sense of satisfaction with the relationship. Provided the channels of communication remain open, conflicts should remain at a minimum.

There is a key question you should ask yourself whenever a conflict arises in your relationship, "Would this issue matter if I were in the woods, or to a three-year old?" Your answer to this question will help you to ascertain whether or not the source of the conflict is arising from vital life sustaining aspects of your relationship or from a more distant place defined by social or ego pressures? If your answer is yes, recognize that the conflict has the power to destroy your relationship if not resolved satisfactorily. If your answer is no, there is a good chance the conflict may

be less serious and may require an alternative approach to resolution.

E-Type Combination 5/8

Solitary Mystic ♥ Conquistador

General Nature of Your Relationship

The energies within this relationship are complementary, with one partner moving forcefully outward and the other moving inward. Both partners are free spirits and may function independently without causing conflict. Tensions are usually resolved by the Conquistador's directness in exploring issues and the Solitary Mystic's ability to quietly dissect and reveal underlying causes and effects. The Conquistador brings the partner out of self-imposed exile, while the Solitary Mystic provides a safe harbor for regeneration and the free exchange of ideas and information.

Primary Sources of Conflict

Conflict arises when the extreme nature of these two personalities become activated. One partner can become overly dominant and controlling while the other can become distant to the point of being emotionally absent. The Conquistador needs confrontation to resolve conflicts but ends up shadow boxing. Under extreme duress these partners can move in opposite directions for very long periods of time without resolving the sources of conflict. "I don't want to talk about it." "Suit yourself. I'm out of here." When the showdown finally arrives, two strong-willed participants engage in protracted and fiery encounters that eventually end in peaceful reconciliation.

Recommended Courses of Action

There are complementary attributes existent within this relationship. The Conquistador exhibits boldness of action, which can benefit the Solitary Mystic. The Solitary Mystic offers deep thinking and emotional restraint, thus benefiting the Conquistador. "I want to pull you out of your shell." "I want to slow you down." The best course of action for this couple is to never lose sight of the special qualities of the relationship and savor the quiet moments together.

There is a key question you should ask yourself whenever a conflict arises in your relationship, "Would this issue matter if I were in the woods, or to a three-year old?" Your answer to this question will help you to ascertain whether or not the source of the conflict is arising from vital life sustaining aspects of your relationship or from a more distant place defined by social or ego pressures? If your answer is yes, recognize that the conflict has the power to destroy your relationship if not resolved satisfactorily. If your answer is no, there is a good chance the conflict may be less serious and may require an alternative approach to resolution.

E-Type Combination 5/9

Solitary Mystic   Harmonizer

General Nature of Your Relationship

The Solitary Mystic needs freedom to pursue interests without a great deal of interruption or interference, while the Harmonizer needs to feel emotionally connected to the partner, family and friends. One partner is independent, while the other is dependent upon the actions and approval of others. One partner moves toward others in order to define identity, while the other moves away from others to protect privacy. One partner is energized by social contact, while the other is drained by it. A successful union is usually sustained by a transcendent commitment. "You are everything I want and everything I need. I will never leave you."

Primary Sources of Conflict

The primary source of conflict in this relationship occurs when the Harmonizer tries to involve the Solitary Mystic in outside activities. One partner needs these activities to feel alive and connected while the other does not. This often results in these partners living separate lives. One partner becomes angry at the seeming lack of support, while the other feels repelled by the thought of wasting time. "You never want to go anywhere." "I don't want to go and be bored to death." This can lead to conflict, given that a compromise requires one partner to 'grin and bear it'.

Recommended Courses of Action

Social occasions are seen as meaningful to one partner and meaningless to the other. If the Solitary Mystic must frequently endure long, drawn out affairs of little interest, conflicts will likely endure. If the Harmonizer must frequently function without a partner, there will be a diminishment of satisfaction and feelings of abandonment. One partner may be perceived as selfish while the other appears shallow. It is essential that this couple work through these differences. "I will go alone to this event, but you come with me to the play on Saturday." "Let's both go, but we will only stay for two hours unless you want to stay longer."

There is a key question you should ask yourself whenever a conflict arises in your relationship, "Would this issue matter if I were in the woods, or to a three-year old?" Your answer to this question will help you to ascertain whether or not the source of the conflict is arising from vital life sustaining aspects of your relationship or from a more distant place defined by social or ego pressures? If your answer is yes, recognize that the conflict has the power to destroy your relationship if not resolved satisfactorily. If your answer is no, there is a good chance the conflict may

be less serious and may require an alternative approach to resolution.

E-Type Combination 6/6

Closet Rebel   Closet Rebel

General Nature of Your Relationship

This union has a 'you and me against the world' feel to it. Both partners are attracted to causes where their natural skepticism may be applied. This couple strives for certainty in their relationship and become anxious when the status quo is violated. They both scan the horizon for what could go wrong. Often the smallest deviation sends them reeling until the perceived threat has passed. Their innate skepticism can prevent them from taking risks. The love connection can be strong between these two personalities because of the similarities of their worldviews. It would be very unlikely for this couple to vote for candidates from different political parties.

Primary Sources of Conflict

This couple is more likely to 'die a slow death' than experience a good old-fashioned donnybrook. If sufficient stimulation is lacking in the relationship, over time, a downer effect sets in, or a leaking of the positive energy that is needed for a healthy relationship. This is caused by a shared tendency toward over analysis and general skepticism regarding the future. If a bogeyman is seen around every corner, the relationship loses its fun and adventure. Thus the threat is one of a slow eroding of life energy rather than one of sharp, angry outbursts. "What's there to look forward to?"

Recommended Courses of Action

Because of the natural skepticism, the relationship runs the risk of losing its spark. It is recommended that this couple make it a priority to participate in activities that both partners consider pure, unadulterated fun on a regular basis. Most likely this couple engages in interesting and deeply penetrating discussions. They need to make sure that these conversations end on an upbeat note of confidence rather than with fear and suspicion. "If we stick together we can overcome this."

There is a key question you should ask yourself whenever a conflict arises in your relationship, "Would this issue matter if I were in the woods, or to a three-year old?" Your answer to this question will help you to ascertain whether or not the source of the conflict is arising from vital life sustaining aspects of your relationship or from a more distant place defined by social or ego pressures? If your answer is yes, recognize that the conflict has the power to destroy your relationship if not resolved satisfactorily. If your answer is no, there is a good chance the conflict may be less serious and may require an alternative approach to resolution.

E-Type Combination 6/7

Closet Rebel   Cruise Director

General Nature of Your Relationship

A union of two people with opposing worldviews may characterize this relationship. One partner sees life filled with unlimited and fun-filled possibilities while the other has a more dogged and skeptical approach to life. This creates an interesting force field within the relationship, with one partner pulling outward while the other resists and pulls in the opposite direction. Successful couples recognize these divergent tendencies and agree to compromise. The Closet Rebel learns his Cruise Director partner does not always act on her grandiose plans, while the Cruise Director comes to value the reality check provided by her Closet Rebel partner.

Primary Sources of Conflict

Conflict occurs in this relationship when the Cruise Director spirals into a social orbit that does not take the feelings of her partner into sufficient consideration; this results in increased feelings of anxiety and suspicion by the partner. The Closet Rebel then tries to control or restrict his partner in order to restore the equilibrium of the relationship. The Cruise Director responds by rebelling and harboring feelings of escape.

Recommended Courses of Action

This couple will benefit by keeping the lines of communication open. It is more effective to discuss problems while going for a walk than to conduct marathon discussions of problems around the kitchen table. Also, there needs to be an acknowledgement that compromise must be a central feature of the relationship. The Cruise Director needs excitement and adventure while the Closet Rebel needs reassurance and trust. These partners need to ensure these elements are included as basic building blocks of the relationship.

There is a key question you should ask yourself whenever a conflict arises in your relationship, "Would this issue matter if I were in the woods, or to a three-year old?" Your answer to this question will help you to ascertain whether or not the source of the conflict is arising from vital life sustaining aspects of your relationship or from a more distant place defined by social or ego pressures? If your answer is yes, recognize that the conflict has the power to destroy your relationship if not resolved satisfactorily. If your answer is no, there is a good chance the conflict may be less serious and may require an alternative approach to resolution.

E-Type Combination 6/8

Closet Rebel   Conquistador

General Nature of Your Relationship

In this relationship, one partner serves in the dominant or leadership position, while the other provides insight and valuable support. The Conquistador is bold and headstrong while the Closet Rebel is more methodical and deliberate. These differences can serve as an effective balancing of energies, which prevents the more daring partner from taking excessive risks without adequate consultation and reality checks. Because of these balancing energies, this couple has the potential to become very successful in their endeavors together, provided they stay connected and trust one another's instincts.

Primary Sources of Conflict

The primary source of conflict in this relationship occurs whenever the Conquistador attempts to provide assistance to the partner and this results in the crossing of boundaries of responsibility. "This is my problem, not yours." The

Conquistador's tendency is to take charge and take control of situations that require change, without thinking of the partner's need for a more cautious approach. "I can see exactly what needs to be done." "Fine, but I'll do it in my own way." Conquistadors can lash out if they suspect weakness or insecurity in the partner. "Stop being such a pansy and let's get on with it."

Recommended Courses of Action

At the heart of this relationship are two individuals who supply the critical ingredients for happiness. The Conquistador provides a sense of strength and protection, which are needed by the partner. The Closet Rebel provides the loyalty and reliability essential to their partner. This couple will benefit by increasing interpersonal sensitivity on the part of one partner, which is lacking, while the other partner steps up and becomes a more dominant and assertive force in the relationship, which will take courage. Personal growth is the key to reduction of conflicts in this relationship.

There is a key question you should ask yourself whenever a conflict arises in your relationship, "Would this issue matter if I were in the woods, or to a three-year old?" Your answer to this question will help you to ascertain whether or not the source of the conflict is arising from vital life

sustaining aspects of your relationship or from a more distant place defined by social or ego pressures? If your answer is yes, recognize that the conflict has the power to destroy your relationship if not resolved satisfactorily. If your answer is no, there is a good chance the conflict may be less serious and may require an alternative approach to resolution.

E-Type Combination 6/9

Closet Rebel   Harmonizer

General Nature of Your Relationship

This relationship may be characterized by compatibility and harmony. The Harmonizer provides a safe harbor for the Closet Rebel to dock, thus providing a harmonious family unit. Neither partner places pressure on the other to achieve unattainable goals, which reduces stress and increases feelings of safety and satisfaction. This couple may also enjoy participating in the same types of activities, further reducing the stress on the relationship.

Primary Sources of Conflict

Conflict occurs in this relationship whenever the Harmonizer is perceived to have shut down and become inactive. The Closet Rebel prods the partner to get moving; the partner responds with stubborn refusal. An impasse occurs which increases the doubt and anxiety in the Closet Rebel. "Will you please focus and stop piddling around?" "Stop telling me what to do!" This conflict is experienced more as nagging irritation than outright bursts of anger.

Recommended Courses of Action

The Harmonizer often has difficulty making decisions and actually knowing what he/she wants out of life. Because of this vacillation the partner can appear passive, zoned out and in free-fall. "I don't really know what I want, so how can I act on it? Let's decide what you want and we'll just do that." The Closet Rebel may also have a problem with commitment because of a tendency toward doubt and suspicion. This couple will benefit by recognizing the tendency toward inertia that exists within the relationship and making a commitment to take the initiative and live a more active life. Increased activity results in less conflict within this partnership.

There is a key question you should ask yourself whenever a conflict arises in your relationship, "Would this issue matter if I were in the woods, or to a three-year old?" Your answer to this question will help you to ascertain whether or not the source of the conflict is arising from vital life sustaining aspects of your relationship or from a more distant place defined by social or ego pressures? If your answer is yes, recognize that the conflict has the power to destroy your relationship if not resolved satisfactorily. If your answer is no, there is a good chance the conflict may be less serious and may require an alternative approach to resolution.

E-Type Combination 7/7

Cruise Director   Cruise Director

General Nature of Your Relationship

This relationship may be characterized as lightning in a bottle. This couple wants it all and they want it right now; the more fun the better. "Let's keep it light and interesting." At their best these partners are like starbursts illuminating everything around them. They get invited to every party and enliven the social occasions in which they participate. Their life can be viewed as a series of activities strung together by a desire to acquire every experience the world has to give.

Primary Sources of Conflict

There is no anchor in this relationship. Both partners want lift off without any restrictions whatsoever. Anything that is painful to address gets sublimated into a frenzy of activity. "Let's not talk about that right now. How about a bike ride?" Problems have a way of festering until they become so intense that they cannot be ignored. Anything that holds these individuals down or restricts them in any way can become a source of conflict. A long-term commitment may be difficult for these individuals without the establishment of a more realistic sense of life's possibilities.

Recommended Courses of Action

Both partners have a voracious appetite for life experiences, which makes this relationship fun and adventurous. Both individuals resist anything they perceive as boring or restrictive. This perspective can result in a life that just skims along the surface and never dives deeply into the core of issues. This couple can benefit from the realization that avoidance is their favorite defense mechanism, with conflicts not always being adequately addressed. This partnership requires greater introspection and the evoking and processing of possibly stress-inducing topics. The key result will be greater authenticity and a partnership grounded in the bedrock of reality.

There is a key question you should ask yourself whenever a conflict arises in your relationship, "Would this issue matter if I were in the woods, or to a three-year old?" Your answer to this question will help you to ascertain whether or not the source of the conflict is arising from vital life sustaining aspects of your relationship or from a more distant place defined by social or ego pressures? If your answer is yes, recognize that the conflict has the power to destroy your relationship if not resolved satisfactorily. If your answer is no, there is a good chance the conflict may be less serious and may require an alternative approach to resolution.

E-Type Combination 7/8

Cruise Director   Conquistador

General Nature of Your Relationship

This relationship may be characterized by high energy. Both partners are individualistic by nature and require freedom of action to thrive. This couple can achieve a great deal in life and contribute to the well being of others through their extroverted nature and good hearts. These individuals can be passionate lovers of life, wanting to taste the best the world has to offer. There is more than ample compatibility available to this couple, provided there are shared goals within the union.

Primary Sources of Conflict

The primary source of conflict within this relationship has to do with dominance issues. The Conquistador strives to establish dominance, while the Cruise Director pulls the escape hatch. "Stop trying to control me!" "Someone has to!" One partner attempts to provide structure while the other avoids commitment. One partner tries for closure the other wants options. This can result in loud explosions of anger. "You are never there when I need you!" "Why do you need me so much?"

Recommended Courses of Action

Overall this is a highly complementary couple, capable of achieving happiness and satisfaction. These individuals could benefit from the establishment of 'rules of the road' whereby the roles played and the needs of both become clearly established. "When you do that it makes me want to run away." "When you are not available and I need you, it makes me feel as though you don't really love me." This couple is encouraged to engage in more heart to heart discussions, rather than quick settlements and surface forgiveness.

There is a key question you should ask yourself whenever a conflict arises in your relationship, "Would this issue matter if I were in the woods, or to a three-year old?" Your answer to this question will help you to ascertain whether or not the source of the conflict is arising from vital life sustaining aspects of your relationship or from a more distant place defined by social or ego pressures? If your answer is yes, recognize that the conflict has the power to destroy your relationship if not resolved satisfactorily. If your answer is no, there is a good chance the conflict may be less serious and may require an alternative approach to resolution.

E-Type Combination 7/9

Cruise Director ♥ Harmonizer

General Nature of Your Relationship

An interesting and rather peaceful couple may characterize this relationship, with one partner hot on the pursuit of interesting outside activities while the other goes along for the ride. The Harmonizer gets a spark of energy and direction from the Cruise Director, while the Cruise Director gets a willing accomplice more than eager to share all of the exciting adventures life holds in store. One partner thrives on diversity of experience while the other appreciates more of a predictable routine. These energies complement one another, resulting in a potentially harmonious union.

Primary Sources of Conflict

Cruise Directors strive to avoid discomfort, which explains their desire for keeping multiple options open at all times; Harmonizers want to avoid feeling strong negative emotions, which explains their more passive and avoidant behaviors. Problems may not be adequately explored with this couple until those problems become severe. "Let's go visit the kids rather than talk about this." "Ok. I didn't really want to get into it anyway." Conflict can arise when the Cruise Director pursues too many projects and activities while the Harmonizer is feeling the Cruise Director is not carrying an equal share of the load.

Recommended Courses of Action

There is potential for a strong love connection between these two individuals, provided their relationship stays grounded. One partner does not need this grounding as much as the other. This can cause the relationship to get out of equilibrium. This couple would benefit by resolving troublesome issues before they explode into gut-wrenching conflicts. By limiting the size of the issues, both partners can remain in their relative comfort zones, not too distasteful and restricting for the Cruise Director and not too threatening to the Harmonizer.

There is a key question you should ask yourself whenever a conflict arises in your relationship, "Would this issue matter if I were in the woods, or to a three-year old?" Your answer to this question will help you to ascertain whether or not the source of the conflict is arising from vital life sustaining aspects of your relationship or from a more distant place defined by social or ego pressures? If your answer is yes, recognize that the conflict has the power to destroy your relationship if not resolved satisfactorily. If your answer is no, there is a good chance the conflict may be less serious and may require an alternative approach to resolution.

E-Type Combination 8/8

Conquistador   Conquistador

General Nature of Your Relationship

This relationship can be fraught with fireworks. Both partners may be combative and self-centered. Conflict and anger do not arouse fear or anxiety within this couple; arguments are often used as a means to clear the air and get to the truth. Usually, one of these partners flexes into a more genteel mode, because the relationship could not be sustained with two dominant Conquistador spouses. There also can be great intimacy and closeness between this couple, evoking the image of two individuals kissing in the middle of a minefield. A friend may say, "That was a brutal fight you just had with your partner," which elicits the response, "Why? It wasn't that bad."

Primary Sources of Conflict

Conflicts arise within this relationship whenever an unstoppable force meets an immovable object. Conflicts are experienced as brief interludes of boisterous anger, and then it's over. Usually these tensions arise when both partners want their own way and find themselves at an impasse. When one partner is not willing to back down intense anger is expressed, which might be followed by a sudden willingness to compromise.

Recommended Courses of Action

Conquistadors can be very kind-hearted toward others, particularly when they feel secure. Usually they project their power outward in an attempt to create change, with little thought as to how they are coming across to others. Because of their directness, Conquistadors can create anxiety in others without ever knowing it. This couple could benefit from gaining greater self-awareness and reflecting more on how their actions impact others.

There is a key question you should ask yourself whenever a conflict arises in your relationship, "Would this issue matter if I were in the woods, or to a three-year old?" Your answer to this question will help you to ascertain whether or not the source of the conflict is arising from vital life sustaining aspects of your relationship or from a more distant place defined by social or ego pressures? If your answer is yes, recognize that the conflict has the power to destroy your relationship if not resolved satisfactorily. If your answer is no, there is a good chance the conflict may

be less serious and may require an alternative approach to resolution.

E-Type Combination 8/9

Conquistador   Harmonizer

General Nature of Your Relationship

This relationship may be characterized as possessing complementary energies, with one partner providing bold leadership while the other provides needed support. The Conquistador provides the energy and direction required to energize the partner, while the Harmonizer brings the comfort and security so essential to the Conquistador. Each individual brings out the best in the other. If this marriage were a house, the Conquistador would be the roof and the Harmonizer the foundation.

Primary Sources of Conflict

This relationship suffers conflict when the Conquistador feels threatened and loses a sense of security. "If you really loved me, why weren't you there when I needed you?" Under stress the Conquistador moves forcefully to confront problems, which is often interpreted by the partner as invasive, excessive and threatening. This causes the Harmonizer to react with stubborn resistance, or to create distance from the perceived threat. This, in turn, further hurts and angers the partner and the conflict lingers or escalates in intensity.

Recommended Courses of Action

The Harmonizer tends to avoid painful emotions by either ignoring them or becoming so busy that they go unattended. The Conquistador, whose forceful nature could be interpreted as pushy, overbearing and self-centered, tends not to be overly concerned about the perceptions of others. The orientation toward the partner may be, "I only care what you think. No one else matters." Because of the mutually supportive nature of this union, it would be very beneficial for both spouses to clearly identify, and make a special effort to accommodate, one another's innermost

183

needs while participating in activities that increase their respective self-awareness.

There is a key question you should ask yourself whenever a conflict arises in your relationship, "Would this issue matter if I were in the woods, or to a three-year old?" Your answer to this question will help you to ascertain whether or not the source of the conflict is arising from vital life sustaining aspects of your relationship or from a more distant place defined by social or ego pressures? If your answer is yes, recognize that the conflict has the power to destroy your relationship if not resolved satisfactorily. If your answer is no, there is a good chance the conflict may be less serious and may require an alternative approach to resolution.

E-Type Combination 9/9

Harmonizer   Harmonizer

General Nature of Your Relationship

This relationship evokes the image of a shimmering lake at twilight – nothing but peacefulness and quietude. The connection between this couple can be so strong that they may finish one another's sentences, enjoy the same activities and share similar likes and dislikes. Overall this is a placid union wherein both partners shun conflict and place a priority on sharing and comfort.

Primary Sources of Conflict

The primary source of conflict within this partnership has to do with dominance and leadership. These individuals are more comfortable adapting to the needs of others than establishing priorities, facing troublesome issues and providing the push to get things done. It may be extremely frustrating for both partners when nothing is decided and goals aren't acted upon. Rather than explosive conflict, this couple can experience "dead space" in their relationship, with both waiting for the other to take charge and provide the initiative. "Are we wasting our time here?" "Tell me what you want." "I don't know what I want." "I don't know what I want either."

Recommended Courses of Action

There is no catalyst within this relationship, therefore it would be very beneficial for this couple to set priorities and assign responsibilities for carrying them out. This action plan should be based upon the interests and aptitudes of each spouse. "You meet with the insurance agent by Friday and I will pick up the gift for your mother by then as well." Providing structure to this union will go a long way toward keeping the peace.

There is a key question you should ask yourself whenever a conflict arises in your relationship, "Would this issue matter if I were in the woods, or to a three-year old?" Your answer to this question will help you to ascertain whether or not the source of the conflict is arising from vital life sustaining aspects of your relationship or from a more distant place defined by social or ego pressures? If your answer is yes, recognize that the conflict has the power to destroy your relationship if not resolved satisfactorily. If your answer is no, there is a good chance the conflict may

be less serious and may require an alternative approach to resolution.

Chapter 5

Between a Man and a Woman

What counts in making a happy marriage is not so much how compatible you are, but how you deal with incompatibility.

— Leo Tolstoy

The unique areas of potential conflict that exist between you and your spouse are intrinsic aspects of your essence, or core expressions of your identity. You are not going to substantially change your expression of being simply because you think it will reduce tension in your marriage. That is not a viable option. Many couples intuitively understand this basic truth and often come to the conclusion that there is no way to reconcile their differences. However, all is not lost. I ask you to remember that your heart invited your spouse into your life when it could have easily sent strong negative signals that would have been difficult for you to ignore. What does the heart know that you don't?

The energy field of the heart is tapped into knowledge that is outside of your awareness. What appears to you to be confounding or impossible is meaningless to the heart because its knowledge is transcendent, it does not rely on logic but on truth. Unless your decision to marry was based on ego, your heart knows the potential for personal growth and happiness exists within your relationship. It took a peek inside your partner and said, "Yes."

Some couples believe that if their partners were truly soul mates, coexistence would be effortless, and that conflict is a sign the relationship is star-crossed. "If I had married the right person we would not be having so much trouble getting along." Let me reiterate a statement made in the previous paragraph: the heart knows what you need, both for happiness and growth. Seldom does growth occur without obstacles, effort, frustration and diligence. Often conflict is so painful it forces you to take a hard look at yourself. "Am I at fault?" "Is there some aspect of me I need to change?" "Am I being too rigid?" The pain can become so intense at times if feels as though it is occurring deep within the soul. This periodic abrasion or rub between two personalities often creates the energy and motivation that is required for the couple's personal growth. "No one can irritate me the way you can." "Ditto."

Because this book is primarily for those who are either retired or about to retire, most likely you have been successful in maintaining a long-term marriage. You might say that your combined personalities have marinated for quite some time now. That is why marital conflict at this stage of life comes as such a surprise. No one expects it to occur. One day everything is going along as usual and then, out of the blue, conflicts and tension arise at shorter and shorter intervals. "What happened to us? We used to be so happy."

Outward expressions of love tend to diminish over time. Think back to when you were first married. How often did you kiss your spouse? How about now? How often did you tell your partner you loved him? How about now? How often did you give your spouse a compliment? How about now?

Over the years ardor declines; this is a natural process. Long-term marriages are like a good wine: it takes many years for it to ferment and age to perfection. It takes just the right ingredients, as well as an optimum environment in which to transform into a most select state. Over time love becomes more subtle and abstract. It is expressed less often in overt actions and more in small gestures and quiet moments of appreciation. This is a natural evolution brought on by time and familiarity. When conflict arises, it is like removing the cork from the cask. It introduces a foreign element that is not conducive to the quality of the end product, and needs immediate attention. Long-term relationships clearly undergo subtle changes that are inevitable and multidimensional. Often we are not completely aware of these changes because they are evolutionary by nature.

Do you really know what your spouse finds most compelling about you? What characteristics do you possess that your spouse finds most attractive? What does your spouse appreciate the most about you? Let's check your assumptions now.

On the following pages you will find twenty-five sentence completion items titled "Between a Man" and the same number for "... and a Woman." Remove these pages from the book by cutting along the dotted line at the margin. The male member of the couple is to receive the "Between a Man" pages while the female member receives "... and a Woman" pages. Separately and in complete privacy, complete each sentence in reference to your spouse. If you thought your partner had beautiful hair, you may complete the following sentence, "What I like best about your physical appearance ... (answer) is the color and texture of your hair."

After you have completed all sentence completion items, once again in complete privacy, share your answers with your spouse. Start with the first item, share your answers, and then comment or discuss them as required. Do this for all the sentence completion items that follow. Have fun with this exercise and enjoy the enlightening communication that ensues. Since there may be intimate information shared during this experience, it is recommended you either destroy these pages, or keep them in a secure and private place, at the end of your session.

Between a Man ...

1. Every time I touch you I ...

2. When I look into your eyes I see ...

3. The physical trait I like best about you is ...

4. The first time I saw you I thought ...

5. You make me laugh when ...

6. I feel love when you ...

Between a Man ...

| 7. What I appreciate most about you is ...

✂

|

|

| 8. If I could do your portrait, I would emphasize
| your ...

✂

|

|

| 9. I feel your strength when you ...

|

✂

|

| 10. Thank you for supporting me when ...

|

|

✂

| 11. I feel closest to you when ...

|

|

|

✂

|

Between a Man ...

12. I am so happy that you ...

13. I realize you sacrificed for me when you ...

14. I feel joy when you ...

15. I love to talk to you about ...

16. If I could write a book about you it would be called ...

17. I feel important whenever you...

Between a Man ...

18. You have good taste in ...

19. I wish that you ...

20. I am sorry that ...

21. Through it all you have been ...

22. I wish you would forgive me for ...

23. Our time together has been ...

Between a Man ...

24. No one knows that ...

25. If I could do it over again I would ...

...**And a Woman**

1. Every time I touch you I ...

2. When I look into your eyes I see ...

3. The physical trait I like best about you is ...

4. The first time I saw you I thought ...

5. You make me laugh when ...

6. I feel love when you ...

...**And a Woman**

7. What I appreciate most about you is ...

8. If I could do your portrait, I would emphasize your ...

9. I feel your strength when you ...

10. Thank you for supporting me when ...

11. I feel closest to you when ...

12. I am so happy that you ...

...**And a Woman**

| 13. I realize you sacrificed for me when you ...

|

|

|

✂ 14. I feel joy when you ...

|

|

|

| 15. I love to talk to you about ...

✂

|

|

| 16. If I could write a book about you it would be
| called ...

✂

|

|

| 17. I feel important whenever you...

|

✂

|

|

| 18. You have good taste in ...

...**And a Woman**

19. I wish that you ...

20. I am sorry that ...

21. Through it all you have been ...

22. I wish you would forgive me for ...

23. Our time together has been ...

24. No one knows that ...

...**And a Woman**

25. If I could do it over again I would ...

Chapter 6

Looking For Love in All the Wrong Places

To know love we must give it.

— *Take Me to Truth: Nouk Sanchez & Tomas Vieira*

The purpose of the last chapter was to evoke and illuminate those long-held positive feelings you have for your spouse. As you shared your answers, what were you thinking at the time? Did you find this exercise easy or difficult? Possibly it made you a bit uncomfortable expressing your emotions in this fashion, yet in some strange way you may also have experienced a sense of release from the exercise.

Love is not a state of mind, but a state of being. You must have love within you before you can give it to someone else. If you cannot discover the love that is within you, it cannot be transmitted to another. Love grows when it is shared

205

with another person and shrinks when it is withheld. When we feel love we experience divine grace. There is no substitute for love; nothing can replace it in our lives no matter how hard we try to find a surrogate. The reason is that true love is divinity in action, while false love is a product of the ego and lacks authenticity. False love is man-made while true love is an extension of the spirit. It is possibly best expressed by I Corinthians 13:4-7, 13:

> Love is patient and kind; love is not jealous or boastful it is not arrogant or rude. Love does not insist on its own way; it is not irritable or resentful; it does not rejoice at wrong, but rejoices in the right. Love bears all things, believes all things, hopes all things, endures all things.

Searching for love outside of ourselves is a fool's errand, because it is already within us, the substance from which we are made. If we seek it from friends, family and lovers we will not find it; however, if we give it to those around us without preconditions we will discover it residing within ourselves, a positive force for health and happiness.

Celebrate the love that is already inside you. Giving love enhances the love you feel inside. Love is either expanding or retracting within us at all times; it is not merely dependent upon our romantic interests, but also upon how we decide to live our lives. We are either giving love or waiting for someone to give it to us, which is a judgment error since the spark of love can only be activated within each of us and then transferred outward. You are giving love each time you help someone or show compassion. Anything in our environment that triggers love feelings within us is extremely beneficial to our happiness and wellbeing.

Younger people often search for love outside of themselves, leading to feelings of emptiness and frustration. "Why can't I find that special love?" The lives of older people may feel barren and loveless because they are looking for love in all the wrong places. If you have ever depended upon another person as the main source of your happiness, you know what I mean.

False Love

False love is created by the ego, which is the sense of self that was created in our childhood. It is always asking for recognition and appreciation. That's why we continuously ask for attention. When controlled by the ego, you get the idea of who you are from others. It is not a direct experience, but the opinions of others—or your perception of those opinions—that shape what you accept as your true identity. This assumed identity is very frail because it lacks a connection to your true self. It craves specialness and appreciation because it is the food of the ego, and its appetite is insatiable. When it does not feel these qualities its existence becomes threatened. A clinical psychologist friend once told me that at the core of many marital difficulties he encounters in his practice is the sense that one of the partners does not feel *special* within the relationship. In other words, one of the spouses is not made to feel unique, exceptional, extraordinary or distinctive by the other. These are all requirements of the ego and place a terrible burden on a marriage.

If the ego is the dominant force in your life it opens the door to misery, because it is reliant upon other people for its identity. It is split off from divine energy and therefore seeks to be special, which means separate. This distinctiveness is essential to the ego because that is how it defines itself. Its boundaries are established by carving out a distinct, yet weak and vulnerable niche that is highly susceptible to threats from the outside. Any form of perceived rejection can be a crushing blow to the ego. Alternatively, whenever we meet the demands of the ego and experience the initial flood of euphoria, it is surprising how unfulfilling and empty it feels over time.

The ego must extract its needs from the outside environment, therefore, it will have a tendency to influence love decisions based on attributes that enhance its image, secretly thinking, "If I marry that beautiful girl it will make me look good to the guys at the club." "If I had that car people would notice me." "I want to win this election so everyone will know how special I am." Of course, attaining all of these goals may be pleasant in the short term, but none of them are capable of filling the deep-seated need for true love that remains unsatisfied within. This creates a vicious cycle of frantic striving to acquire ego-boosting assets, only to experience hollowness and disappointment once they are acquired.

True Love

True love is the goal of almost every person on earth, but very few people really know how to obtain it. Some confuse sexual attraction with true love, while others feel that a strong emotional attachment is the real thing. Neither of these fulfills the criteria of true love because they are temporary attractions that usually diminish over time or become volatile and capricious. True love is based on the following elements:

- There are no preconditions
- It is not a special quality

- It is based on freedom

- It is enduring and eternal

- It is for the benefit of others

- It has unison of purpose

There are no preconditions.

There is no if/then loop with true love. One never thinks "If you do this for me I will do that for you." True love is simply an expression of divinity with no quid pro quos. "I love you because I love you. It doesn't matter what I receive in return." There is no 'I' in true love because it is not about separation, but integration. Giving is the authentic expression of true love, while taking is the expression of false love. One never thinks, "What's in this for me?" One always thinks, "What's in this for us?"

It is not a special quality.

True love is an intrinsic aspect of who we are as spiritual beings. It is not something we obtain from the outside world as some special dispensation. Whenever we are connected to our essence, the source of love, it becomes a natural and free flowing energy that touches everyone and everything around us. It is within all of us at all times.

It is based on freedom.

The nature of false love is grasping and controlling, while true love is based on freedom and liberation. The spirit of true love is not about getting, but about giving. How can a relationship evolve and grow without the freedom to pursue change? Severe restrictions in a relationship are based on the insecurity of the ego: the threat of losing its source of specialness. Freedom is also given so that we may work through life's challenges and difficulties and encounter our own strengths and weaknesses. Love grants the freedom to succeed or fail.

It is enduring and eternal.

True love is not of this earth, but is transcendent and everlasting. It is not transient, nor dependent upon anyone's actions. It is ethereal. It has no bounds. If a long-term relationship comes to a crashing end, chances are it was occupied by one or more egos competing for attention, not true love. If you have ever looked into the heart of your spouse or child and felt nothing but pure love, you have been touched by the experience. Love becomes embellished when it is an authentic expression of your essence. The more you love the more you feel love. Love is diminished when it becomes contaminated by the desires of the ego.

It is for the benefit of others.

True love is a selfless expression. It requires nothing in return. It is a spiritual outreach or extension of loving energy toward another. It is 'other centric', meaning it is expressed for the specific purpose of helping or supporting another being. When this approach is reciprocal there is unshakable harmony in a relationship. In these types of relationships, it brings out the best in both partners; it challenges them to grow and improve; it encourages them to be more giving and balanced in their attitude toward life; it strengthens their bond with spiritual energy.

It has unison of purpose.

True love has a transcendent quality that may be stated or unstated between the partners in the marriage. This quality has adhering elements that bind the spouses to the purpose. It may be spiritual evolution, mental health, charitable causes, family support, fundraising or religious faith. Whatever the purpose may be, the couple tends to make a commitment to the cause and organizes their relationship toward its attainment because it brings positive energy into their lives. On the charitable side, I think of the Shriver family and its commitment to those with special needs, Danny Thomas' commitment to St. Jude's Hospital and Bill and Melinda Gates' commitment to charitable giving, all involving extended family members. Whatever the purpose, it offers a unifying quality to the relationship that promotes the welfare and personal growth of both partners.

Challenges in a True Love Relationship

Even when a couple's marriage is fundamentally a true love relationship, this does not mean there will never be conflict within the marriage. It does mean, however, that the relationship is supported by what is real rather than what is false. This provides the underlying strength and cohesion required to withstand the severe trials life may bring. "Together we can get through anything."

Compatibility and happiness need to be created within the union, they do not just automatically appear out of nowhere. Happiness results as a product of interactions between the partners – a series of reconciliations and accommodations whereby adjustments are constantly being made for the benefit of the union as a cohesive unit. Inside each of us is an urge toward wholeness, or a compelling drive for personal and spiritual growth. This is what creates the momentum for the relationship to grow and prosper: achievement of what is real and authentic, and not what is false and artificial.

Conflict cannot be resolved on the level of the ego because the ego has no underlying structure. There is no there there. Buying a new house will not solve marital conflicts, nor will gifting expensive jewelry, because such actions do not get at the root of the conflict. At best they provide a temporary reprieve, but little of lasting value.

Conflict resolution within true love relationships offers significant opportunities for personal growth. When the equilibrium is disturbed by conflict, here are some questions you can ask that may yield positive results.

- What is the role of the ego in this conflict?
- How can I engage in this conflict without offending or hurting my partner or myself?
- How can I find the truth in this conflict?
- How can the resolution of this conflict be reciprocal?
- How can the strengthening of our union be the outcome of this conflict?

What is the role of the ego?

It is essential to ferret out any ego contamination that may be the cause of a conflict. The ego never goes away and may be discovered lurking in the background, waiting for the opportunity to resurface and influence events. At best it can be neutralized, but not eliminated. Is the tension being created by what other people think? Is anyone's image being threatened in any way? Often just the recognition of the ego's involvement in the discord leads to a positive resolution of the conflict.

How can I engage in this conflict without offending or hurting my partner or myself?

Maintaining the integrity of the family unit is an important goal in conflict resolution, no matter how intense the disagreement. What will be left standing after this conflict gets resolved? A 'scorched earth' approach to conflict usually results in loss of trust and long-term damage to the relationship. The goal is not to win the battle but to resolve the conflict to the benefit of both parties. It is possible to disagree inside of a love relationship without losing one's commitment to the union and the partners who are involved. The Golden Rule applies here: never do or say anything to your partner that you would not want them to do or say to you.

How can I find the truth in this conflict?

Finding the truth is the only way to permanently resolve conflicts; the truth does not reside within the ego, therefore one must look elsewhere for the wellspring of the problem. Discovering the truth should not be threatening because it provides the only true light that can illuminate the underlying causes of the breach. The truth cannot be avoided or camouflaged, only addressed. If ignored it will remain obscured, the true source of the tension will not be revealed, and permanent resolution of the conflict will not be possible.

How can the resolution of this conflict be reciprocal?

Conflict resolution should never be viewed as a win/lose contest. By winning you lose. The overall commitment to the union should always take precedence over temporary or fleeting disagreements. Never lose sight of the feelings of your partner while working out problems; also never permit the violation of your own integrity, or sense of self. There should be no casualties in conflict resolution, only mutual agreement.

How can the strengthening of our union be the outcome of this conflict?

As surprising as it may seem, conflicts can strengthen the union in a true love relationship. Often the air gets cleared of the lingering emotions that were an aspect of the conflict and the way becomes open for a permanent resolution. If the conflict created emotional separation, then the resolution can draw the couple together in a much stronger fashion. When trust is maintained during the conflict, the strength of commitment to the relationship is enhanced. "We can argue but we will still love one another when it's over."

One cannot find love by looking outside of oneself. One cannot give love if one does not find it within first. Love becomes energized and activated when it is given to another. Therefore, if you cannot find love or you feel the love you currently possess is lacking, extend love wherever and whenever you can. Create opportunities by helping others. Those who work in hospice organizations are a good example. One would think they would be negative and depressed; however, you find people with bright energy in their eyes, renewed by their purpose and extension of comfort and love to those who desperately need it. Love is transformative by nature and penetrates every cell in our bodies. It is paradoxical that the more of it you give away the more of it you possess.

Chapter 7

Living in the Flow

It is not correct to say that life is moving,
but life is movement itself.

— Walpola Rahula

When a fish swims in water it has no conscious awareness of the characteristics of water: water just is, passing through it leaves no indelible mark or trace. When a bird flies through the air it has no conscious awareness of the characteristics of the air: air just is, passing through it leaves no indelible mark or trace. Yet water to a fish and air to a bird are the most important elements in their lives. Without these essentials they would perish or suffer a debilitated future.

If a fish were to awaken to the characteristics of water it might alter its behavior and swim closer to the surface or deeper in the depths in order to avoid predators. It might seek warmer water or greater purity or salinity. In fact, increased awareness creates options of response that may lead to improved health and overall wellbeing for the enlightened fish. If the bird were to also awaken to the nature of air, it might fly higher or make better use of the updraft of thermal air currents thus enjoying more effortless flight. It might even decide to fly south earlier in the year. Based on our analogy, becoming more knowledgeable of the natural laws that are in effect in the atmosphere in which one lives can lead to greater control and adaptability and may yield an improved quality of life.

The question arises, what is the human equivalent of water and air? What is the immediate environment in which we swim or fly? Are there universal laws that exist in the atmosphere of human existence that may guide us in making more informed decisions about our life and relationships?

What could be called our water and air is something called the Zero-Point Field. We live in a vibratory world consisting of numerous energy fields. Every cell in our body and every thought in our heads emit a vibratory frequency. Underlying everything you see, touch or perceive is vibratory energy, which is created by energy exchanges. Supporting all of these smaller energy fields is the mother of all energy fields, which is called The Zero-Point Field.

Since it is the lowest energy state it is completely unobservable. It is everywhere inside and outside of us, permeating every atom in our bodies. Everything in your life moves through its presence without you being aware of it. In addition, scientists believe that everything in the universe is interconnected by waves, which move through time and space, making every element in existence interconnected in some small way. As Lynne McTaggart states, "The Zero Point Field is a kind of shadow of the universe for all time, a mirror image and record of everything that ever was."[13]

Everything in your world, no matter how large or small, is fundamentally a collection of electrical charges at the subatomic level that exchange energy with a wide array of other electromagnetic fields. This is important because you emit a personal vibratory frequency that represents a composite of your actions, thoughts and beliefs that influences every relationship you have in your life.

> The deepest state is the highest; the calmest is the most accelerated; the most intimate, loving, connected feelings are the most effective. Love is

---

[13] *The Field,* Lynne McTaggart, Harper Collins, New York, 2002, pg. 26.

> the most motivating and creative frequency of all.
> Truth is love moving through your mind. Harmony
> is love's resonance coordinating and attuning all
> life's vibrations. [14]

Your personal frequency is not static, but dynamic in nature, and is based not only on your own actions and beliefs but by those of people who are close to you as well, such as family members, co-workers, friends and acquaintances. The higher your frequency, the more love is projected from your heart and the stronger the attractor field you send outward toward others. You will attract those who operate on or near your frequency and make those who are far below your frequency uncomfortable. This is why most married couples resonate on the same relative frequency, because of the self-selection process that operates within the attractor field.

How you choose to function in life determines your interaction with the Zero-Point Field. It can be indeterminate or a transformational influence, depending upon your understanding of its nature and the contour of your actions. Physicists postulate it can materialize any potential and is restrained only by our lack of

---

[14] *Frequency,* Penny Peirce, Atria Books, New York, 2009, pg. 51.

understanding of its immense power to bring about positive change. Therefore the goal is to operate in confluence with the energy of this prime field, and not obstruct its enabling properties by the disparity of our actions and life choices.

The Zero-Point Field responds in accordance with our frequency level: the higher the frequency the greater the confluence with the field. It is not composed of inert intelligence, but offers an active potential of all knowledge ever created, or that will ever be created. An action from this field could result in something akin to a miracle, or simply to an increased sense of peace and contentment, all depending upon the intent expressed by the frequency of the interaction and whether or not the right conditions are in place for the change to occur.

The Zero-Point Field's effects are usually extremely subtle, yet enabling by nature. When operating from the ego's perspective, one's energy runs contrary to this field and a negative polarity becomes established; when this occurs life becomes disjointed and is experienced as a struggle. This field is all-encompassing in its function and is based on fundamental truth: the divine glue that holds the universe together.

As surprising as it may seem, an enlightened sage by the name of Lao Tzu who lived in China over 2,500 years ago created the most comprehensive description of the workings of the Zero Point Field, only he called it the Tao. As legend has it, the King of Zhou in Luoyang appointed him Keeper of the Imperial Archives. He studied the archives' books diligently until his wisdom and insight grew and he became a well-known sage throughout the realm.

As time passed Lao Tzu believed the kingdom was about to disintegrate into chaos and decided to depart. He was traveling west on an ox when he came to the Han Gu Pass, which was guarded by the Commander of the Pass and his guards. The Commander recognized the old master and observed that he was leaving permanently.

Because of Lao Tzu's reputation as a great wisdom teacher of the Tao, he insisted that he have tea with him in his office before traveling on to his destination. During the conversation the Commander implored Lao Tzu to write down instructions describing how to live in accordance with the Tao so that his wisdom would not be lost to future generations. Lao Tzu agreed and began working on the document. Once it was completed he handed it over to the Commander and departed, never to be seen or heard from again.

The document, titled *Tao te Ching,* consists of 81 brief chapters or sections. It is considered the most profound wisdom book ever written, a masterpiece that describes the natural laws governing existence, and a philosophical representation of the energy effects of the Zero Point Field. The *Tao* te *Ching* is one of the most translated books of all time.

The wisdom contained in this book offers clear guidelines for us to follow if we want to live a life of tranquility and peace. I must warn you that it presents concepts that are fundamentally counter-intuitive, often challenging the beliefs and influences of our modern culture.

The Tao permeates our existence, there is no escaping its effects upon us. When we live in accordance with the Tao our life seems to flow effortlessly; when we behave contrary to the Tao conflicts and unhappiness eventually arise. There are clear and specific ways of being that place you into the flow of the Tao; as well, there are actions you may take that place you in diametric opposition to the way of the Tao. As you process through this next section I would ask you to think about your relationship. Are you living in accordance with the Tao? If not, what changes do you need to make in your personal behavior and your marriage?

Aligning with the Flow

The Tao encompasses all, not only spirituality but material things as well. It is the manifestation of the prime energy field that defies description. We are constantly exchanging information with the Tao at all times. We cannot approach it with the intellect; we must relate to its energy. It is not possible to gain an analytical understanding of its operation. It requires intuitive insight into the unseen but all-pervasive movement of the field. Lao Tzu called it a mystery. The only way to fully understand it is to experience its effects. The simplest way to grasp it is to accept the notion that there are unseen universal laws that manage reality, and it is highly beneficial to live in harmony with these laws rather than contrary to them.

Behaving in accordance with the Tao can have an immensely positive effect upon your marriage and other relationships, because it reduces stress. But first you must align yourself with this energy field.

Lao Tzu offered a set of general recommendations for those who desire to live within the positive influences of the Tao. What follows is a set of guidelines designed to help you and your partner create a behavioral inventory to determine how closely you are both functioning in accordance with the

Tao. I suggest you use a five-point scale with '5' representing full behavioral adherence to the guideline, and '1' representing a total absence of the behavior in your life. For example, if the suggestion were to live a life full of compassion for your fellow man, your assessment would range from 5 (do it all the time) to 1 (never do it). If you did it some of the time your rating may be a '2' or '3'. Your assessment is dependent upon your self-observation. Write these numbers in the spaces provided following each section. Once completed it is essential that you discuss the ratings with your partner.

1. Manage Your Relationship with a Light Touch

This first recommendation received a great deal of emphasis by Lao Tzu. Do not attempt to over control or possess your partner. A relationship must have an element of freedom within it to be healthy. Be benevolent toward your partner and do not interfere or make a zealous attempt to infuse your beliefs or views. Detaching your emotions is helpful in this regard. Also, it is recommended that you be flexible and adaptable. What is soft and pliable is alive and flexible, what is hard and rigid is dead and lacking energy. Eliminate extremes and be nimble in the face of your relationships and life in general.

_____ Husband   _____Wife

2. Do not Be Overly Calculating in Your Relationship

This is a caution to avoid cleverness, which leads to arrogance. Let the dynamics of your relationship naturally unfold without schemes or hidden control strategies. See your spouse as the manifestation of spiritual energy rather than flesh and blood. Strong desires lead to anxiety and misery. Be thoughtful when engaging in your relationship rather than self-absorbed.

_____ Husband   _____Wife

3. Yield as a Strategy for Handling Conflicts

Yielding does not mean retreating, it means taking a step back. It is not a weak response, but a sign of courage and strength. Avoid being contentious and defensive. By yielding, you afford the time to reposition the conflict away from strong emotions and toward a more rational discussion of issues. Always try to respond with compassion when encountering stressful situations with others. Never seek revenge for perceived offenses.

_____ Husband   _____Wife

4. Do not Keep Emotions Bottled Up

Conflicts are best resolved as they arise, which keeps them in their proper perspective. If they are not addressed immediately, they may cause more and more anger until an explosion occurs. This is not helpful to anyone. The internal pressure created by keeping emotions bottled up can lead to harsh statements and criticisms directed toward your partner that could have been more easily defused if tackled at an earlier stage of development. Negative statements directed toward your partner in the heat of an argument are often difficult to forget and can create distance between you and your spouse.

_____ Husband   _____Wife

5. Be Humble

This is one of the key themes of the Tao and an essential understanding that is required. Lao Tzu speaks of being the valley of the world. He means that all water flows downhill and the streams that are created nurture everything. The energy of the Tao naturally flows to fill up a vacuum. There is power in low places. Showing honest humility is an act of the wise person. It is characterized by showing respect and good will toward others. It is not seeking the limelight or drawing attention to yourself. It is the acknowledgement that living in harmony with the Tao is your locus of power, not the ego.

_____ Husband _____ Wife

6. Live a Life of Moderation

If you are to experience peace and tranquility, you must live a life of simplicity. This requires the removal of complexity wherever it may exist. Focus on your basic needs, which may be more easily attained, and do nothing in excess. Quietness is the goal and moderation is the path. Modern life runs contrary to this guideline. We are pressured in all quarters of our life to accept and manage complexity. Anything that is overly complex is usually not an accurate reflection of the truth. It takes diligent effort and discipline to achieve this goal but this is an essential requirement of the Tao.

_____ Husband _____ Wife

7. Be Helpful

The truth is that by caring for others, you are caring for yourself. Helpfulness is the projection of positive energy. Be selfless by letting go of self-centered thoughts. Whenever being helpful to another, never have strings attached. Always focus on the process and never the outcome. Being helpful is reward in itself. Act without becoming attached to specific outcomes. Focus on the process, not the outcome.

_____ Husband _____Wife

8. Do not Emphasize the Ego

Lao Tzu cautions against any actions that draw attention to the self. It runs contrary to the energy of the Tao. This is seen as a source of dissatisfaction because of the constant fear of disapproval and the negative judgment of others. The higher the spiritual vibration the weaker the energy that is invested in the ego because there is a realization that it is an artificially created self, not your true self.

_____ Husband _____Wife

9. Do not Focus on Material Things

Striving for material things offers diminishing returns once you have secured the basics of life. Often our striving limits the opportunity for serenity and quietude. We must make time to realize these life-enriching rhythms so that we remain balanced and secure. Excessive ambition steals away the opportunity for quiet joy and replaces it with excessive effort, craving and acquisition, which do not usually make us happy in the end.

_____ Husband   _____Wife

10. Accept Reality as it Is

The alternative to accepting reality is making the constant comparison to what reality could be, which keeps us in a constant state of turmoil and arousal. Thinking and judging what could be or should be is comparing present reality to a dream world created by the imagination. Wishing for a better alternative without making the necessary effort for change leads to dissatisfaction. Reality is a momentary truth and exists in its current state for a reason. It requires an element of acceptance before it yields to change.

_____ Husband   _____Wife

11. Focus on Learning from Life's Experiences

Lao Tzu considers learning based on experience to be superior to book learning, which is more of an abstraction. Real experience is the best teacher because it actually happened in real life: it was an authentic outcome that may be observed and evaluated. Real life experience is truthful and cannot be manipulated by cleverness and articulate persuasion. Arrogance is often the outcome of book learning, while real experience can be humbling and point the way to authentic learning based on the bedrock of reality.

_____ Husband _____ Wife

12. Break Large Tasks into Small Parts

Nothing can be accomplished by flying head first into a large task. Small, incremental achievements result in one large accomplishment over time. For example, if you had the discipline to write just one page of text each day, you could publish a book every year. This is an important guide point for your relationship. Do not try to solve all problems at one time, but go slowly and focus on incremental progress. Have patience and diligently tackle smaller aspects of the problem until it is resolved.

_____ Husband _____ Wife

13. Focus on the Essence, not the Veneer

Every challenge in life possesses an inner truth and an artificial truth. The inner truth is what's real and authentic and can lead you to resolution, while the artificial truth is a surface image and offers no real value. Spend no time on the image of things, look to the essence or underlying truth that resides beneath. This is also a caution to avoid the illusions of the world. Be serious and look for the truth in all things. Only there you will find the insights required for effective solutions and decision-making.

_____ Husband   _____Wife

14. Flow Like Water

The Tao is often referred to as the Watercourse Way because Lao Tzu uses water as a constant metaphor throughout the document. He sees water as a useful example of the Tao because of its flowing nature, which nurtures all of life. Water can take any form, is soft and pliable yet can wear away the hardest of stone. Water finds its way around obstacles without permanently altering its character; it takes no credit for its actions and possesses no expectations regarding the outcome. It simply flows and abides by its intrinsic nature.

_____ Husband   _____Wife

Now that you have reviewed these guidelines, compare your evaluations to those of your spouse. Discuss any areas of agreement or disagreement. Your low scores can identify areas for self reflection and help point the way toward improving the overall health of your relationship. Take this challenge seriously and make a commitment to change your behavior if you feel it is required. You may discover that your actions will feel more like the removal of stubborn obstacles than the addition of new personal behaviors. You could even feel a sense of liberation as the changes slowly take effect.

The Way

As we go through life we are confronted by our own natural tendencies that may not always contribute to our happiness. This is how humans are made: a fusion of competing energies struggling for expression. From whence they arise we can only speculate. But when it comes to relationships we do know certain things. We know the heart functions as the gateway to our relationships. We know increased self-awareness helps us to make better decisions. We know combining two unique personalities often results in conflict. We know the ego can inject negative energy into our relationships if we are not careful. We know greater understanding of our partner will lessen the potential for tension in our marriage.

We also know everything in our life emits vibratory energy that is our own unique signature to the rest of the world. Although not obvious, the world is made as a receptacle for our unique energy patterns. The more the contour of our energy conforms to the grand vibratory pattern of the universe, the more our lives move with the natural flow rather than against it, and the more peace and tranquility we experience in our relationships.

My recommendation to you is very simple: live the Tao – be the Tao.

Appendix A

The E-Type Questionnaire

Directions: Read the following statements carefully and decide to what extent they accurately describe you. Write the number of your answer choice in the space marked "Score." It is very important to indicate how you see yourself at this moment, not how you once were or how you would like to be.

1. I enjoy solving difficult problems, even in my spare time.

(1) No, not at all

(2) No, not much

(3) Yes, sometimes

(4) Yes, definitely

Score _____

2. I have a romantic nature.

(1) No, not at all

(2) No, not much

(3) Yes, sometimes

(4) Yes, definitely

Score _____

3. I like to create the right image in order to succeed.

(1) No, not at all

(2) No, not much

(3) Yes, sometimes

(4) Yes, definitely

Score _____

4. I have a flair for the dramatic.

(1) No, not at all

(2) No, not much

(3) Yes, sometimes

(4) Yes, definitely

Score _____

5. I like to be alone most of the time.

(1) No, not at all

(2) No, not much

(3) Yes, sometimes

(4) Yes, definitely

Score _____

6. I am the cautious type and am conservative by nature.

(1) No, not at all

(2) No, not much

(3) Yes, sometimes

(4) Yes, definitely

Score _____

7. I have a sunny personality and people like me because I am interesting.

(1) No, not at all

(2) No, not much

(3) Yes, sometimes

(4) Yes, definitely

Score _____

8. I find it difficult being successful without power and control.

(1) No, not at all

(2) No, not much

(3) Yes, sometimes

(4) Yes, definitely

Score _____

9. I tend to procrastinate.

(1) No, not at all

(2) No, not much

(3) Yes, sometimes

(4) Yes, definitely

Score _____

10. In my spare time I like to fix things.

(1) No, not at all

(2) No, not much

(3) Yes, sometimes

(4) Yes, definitely

Score _____

11. I feel disappointment when others do not meet my expectations.

(1) No, not at all

(2) No, not much

(3) Yes, sometimes

(4) Yes, definitely

Score _____

12. I feel comfortable being in charge.

(1) No, not at all

(2) No, not much

(3) Yes, sometimes

(4) Yes, definitely

Score _____

13. I have been accused of being temperamental.

(1) No, not at all

(2) No, not much

(3) Yes, sometimes

(4) Yes, definitely

Score _____

14. I like to dream up new ideas.

(1) No, not at all

(2) No, not much

(3) Yes, sometimes

(4) Yes, definitely

Score _____

15. I am good at identifying things that could go wrong.

(1) No, not at all

(2) No, not much

(3) Yes, sometimes

(4) Yes, definitely

Score _____

16. I like to plan fun-filled outings.

(1) No, not at all

(2) No, not much

(3) Yes, sometimes

(4) Yes, definitely

Score _____

17. Confrontations do not bother me.

(1) No, not at all

(2) No, not much

(3) Yes, sometimes

(4) Yes, definitely

Score _____

18. I have a hard time knowing what I want.

(1) No, not at all

(2) No, not much

(3) Yes, sometimes

(4) Yes, definitely

Score _____

19. Others do not do things as precisely as I do.

(1) No, not at all

(2) No, not much

(3) Yes, sometimes

(4) Yes, definitely

Score _____

20. It is a high priority for me to stay in close touch with friends and family.

(1) No, not at all

(2) No, not much

(3) Yes, sometimes

(4) Yes, definitely

Score _____

21. I enjoy being the center of attention.

(1) No, not at all

(2) No, not much

(3) Yes, sometimes

(4) Yes, definitely

Score _____

22. I feel sad and melancholy a lot of the time.

(1) No, not at all

(2) No, not much

(3) Yes, sometimes

(4) Yes, definitely

Score _____

23. I like to do in-depth research in subjects that interest me.

(1) No, not at all

(2) No, not much

(3) Yes, sometimes

(4) Yes, definitely

Score _____

24. I am not much of a risk taker and like to plan carefully.

(1) No, not at all

(2) No, not much

(3) Yes, sometimes

(4) Yes, definitely

Score _____

25. I seldom feel depressed because there are so many interesting things to do.

(1) No, not at all

(2) No, not much

(3) Yes, sometimes

(4) Yes, definitely

Score _____

26. I charge forward even if I don't know the outcome.

(1) No, not at all

(2) No, not much

(3) Yes, sometimes

(4) Yes, definitely

Score _____

27. I have difficulty making decisions because I see all sides of an issue.

(1) No, not at all

(2) No, not much

(3) Yes, sometimes

(4) Yes, definitely

Score _____

28. I have a tendency to be too self-critical and demanding.

(1) No, not at all

(2) No, not much

(3) Yes, sometimes

(4) Yes, definitely

Score _____

29. I love taking care of children.

(1) No, not at all

(2) No, not much

(3) Yes, sometimes

(4) Yes, definitely

Score _____

30. Being successful is an essential part of my identity.

(1) No, not at all

(2) No, not much

(3) Yes, sometimes

(4) Yes, definitely

Score _____

31. I have a heightened sensitivity to others' emotions.

(1) No, not at all

(2) No, not much

(3) Yes, sometimes

(4) Yes, definitely

Score _____

32. I like exploring new ideas that others may feel are "far-out."

(1) No, not at all

(2) No, not much

(3) Yes, sometimes

(4) Yes, definitely

Score _____

33. I have a hidden rebellious streak that often goes unnoticed.

(1) No, not at all

(2) No, not much

(3) Yes, sometimes

(4) Yes, definitely

Score _____

34. Having excitement in my life is really important to me.

(1) No, not at all

(2) No, not much

(3) Yes, sometimes

(4) Yes, definitely

Score _____

35. Competition brings out the best in me.

(1) No, not at all

(2) No, not much

(3) Yes, sometimes

(4) Yes, definitely

Score _____

36. It is hard for me to say "no."

(1) No, not at all

(2) No, not much

(3) Yes, sometimes

(4) Yes, definitely

Score _____

37. If I don't do it right, I don't do it at all.

(1) No, not at all

(2) No, not much

(3) Yes, sometimes

(4) Yes, definitely

Score _____

38. I am a loving person but have a stubborn streak.

(1) No, not at all

(2) No, not much

(3) Yes, sometimes

(4) Yes, definitely

Score _____

39. I can adapt myself to fit into almost any situation.

(1) No, not at all

(2) No, not much

(3) Yes, sometimes

(4) Yes, definitely

Score _____

40. If I could be anything, I would like to be a successful and passionate artist.

(1) No, not at all

(2) No, not much

(3) Yes, sometimes

(4) Yes, definitely

Score _____

41. I am uncomfortable at most social gatherings.

(1) No, not at all

(2) No, not much

(3) Yes, sometimes

(4) Yes, definitely

Score _____

42. If I like my boss I am a loyal employee.

(1) No, not at all

(2) No, not much

(3) Yes, sometimes

(4) Yes, definitely

Score _____

43. I get easily bored and am attracted to novelty and new experiences.

(1) No, not at all

(2) No, not much

(3) Yes, sometimes

(4) Yes, definitely

Score _____

44. I can intimidate others with my forcefulness.

(1) No, not at all

(2) No, not much

(3) Yes, sometimes

(4) Yes, definitely

Score _____

45. I avoid conflict whenever possible because it makes me uncomfortable.

(1) No, not at all

(2) No, not much

(3) Yes, sometimes

(4) Yes, definitely

Score _____

Answer Key

E-1	Score	E-2	Score	E-3	Score	E-4	Score	E-5	Score	E-6	Score	E-7	Score	E-8	Score	E-9	Score
Q1		Q2		Q3		Q4		Q5		Q6		Q7		Q8		Q9	
10		11		12		13		14		15		16		17		18	
19		20		21		22		23		24		25		26		27	
28		29		30		31		32		33		34		35		36	
37		38		39		40		41		42		43		44		45	
Total		Total		Total		Total		Total		Total		Total		Total		Total	

Using the Answer Key, enter your answer score (1–4) in the score column next to each question. For example, if your score for question 1 were 2, then you would enter a 2 in the score column next to Q1. If your score for question 10 were 3, then you would enter a 3 in the score column next to Q10. After entering all of your answers in the appropriate columns, total each one. Your totals from each column represent your score for each of the nine E-Types.

What is your highest score? If you have a total E-Type score from 18–20, there is a strong possibility that you have identified your correct type. If you have a score from 16–17 there is some possibility that this is your type.

It is not always easy to identify your correct type. Occasionally, it takes some additional deliberation and self-discovery. If you continue to lack confidence in the identification of your E-Type, you may benefit from reading one or more of the books listed in Recommended Reading.

Recommended Reading

For those interested in learning more about the Enneagram, here are some classic introductory texts you may find helpful and interesting.

Daniels, David, and Virginia A. Price. *The Essential Enneagram*. New York: HarperCollins, 2009.

Palmer, Helen. *The Enneagram in Love and Work*. New York: HarperCollins, 1995.

Riso, Don Richard. *Discovering Your Personality Type*. New York: Houghton Mifflin Company, 2003.

———. *Personality Types*. New York: Houghton Mifflin Company, 1996.

———. *Understanding the Enneagram*. New York: Houghton Mifflin Company, 2000.

Riso, Don Richard and Russ Hudson. *The Wisdom of the Enneagram*. New York: Bantam Books, 1999.

Bibliography

Almaas, A.H. *Facets of Unity: The Enneagram of Holy Ideas.* Berkley, CA: Diamond Books, 1998.

Bo Burlingham, "What Am I, if Not My Business?" *Inc.,* November 2010.

Childre, Doc, and Howard Martin. *The Heartmath Solution.* San Francisco, CA: HarperSanFrancisco, 2000.

Godwin, Gail. *Heart: The Story of its Myths and Meanings.* London, UK: Bloomsbury Publishing, 2001.

Grigg, Ray. *The Tao of Relationships.* Atlanta, GA: Humanics Limited, 1988.

Helen Rumbelow, "An Inconvenient Truth About Late-Life Divorce," *Times Online,* June 4 2010, *http://women.timesonline.co.uk/tol/life_and_style/women/relationships/article7143713.ece.*

Hicks, Esther, and Jerry Hicks. *The Vortex: Where the Law of Attraction Assembles All Cooperative Relationships.* Carlsbad, CA: Hay House, 2009.

James, John. *The Great Field: Soul at Play in a Conscious Universe.* Fulton, CA: Elite Books, 2007.

Katherine Rosman, "Mind Meld," *WSJ, September 2010.*

"Kundalini," www.themystica.com/mystica/articles/k/kundalini.html.

Laszlo, Ervin. *Science and the Akashic Field: An Integral Theory of Everything.* Rochester, VT: Inner Traditions, 2007.

Lin, Derek. *Tao te Ching: Annotated and Explained.* Woodstock, VT: Skylight Paths, 2006.

Linda Marks, "The Power of the Heart," HeartPower, 2003, http://www.healingheartpower.com/power-heart.html.

Christine A. Price, "Marriage After Retirement," Ohio State University Extension, http://ohioline.osu.edu/ss-fact/0212.html.

Maitri, Sandra. *The Spiritual Dimension of the Enneagram: Nine Faces of the Soul.* New York, NY: PenguinPutnam, 2000.

McTaggart, Lynne. *The Field: The Quest for the Secret Force of the Universe.* New York: NY: Harper Collins, 2002.

Osho. *Being in Love: How to Love With Awareness and Relate Without Fear.* New York, NY: Harmony Books, 2008.

Palmer, Helen. *The Enneagram in Love & Work: Understanding Your Intimate & Business Relationships.* New York, NY, HarperCollins, 1995.

Pearce, Joseph Chilton. *The Biology of Transcendence: A Blueprint of the Human Spirit.* Rochester, VT: Park Street Press, 2002. _____. *The Death of Religion and the Rebirth of Spirit: A Return to the Intelligence of the Heart.* Rochester, VT: Park Street Press, 2007.

Peirce, Penney. *Frequency: The Power of Personal Vibration.* New York, NY: Simon & Schuster, 2009.

Rahula, Walpola. *What the Buddha Taught.* New York, NY: Grove Press,1959.

Renard, Gary R. *Your Immortal Reality: How to Break the Cycle of Birth and Death.* New York, NY: Hay House, 2006.

Rollin McCraty, Raymond Trevor Bradley and Dana Tomasino, "The Resonant Heart" Shift: At the Frontiers of Consciousness, December 2004 – February 2005.

Sanchez, Nouk, and Tomas Vieira. *Take Me to Truth: Undoing the Ego.* Olympia, WA: Orca Books, 2007.

Sardello, Robert. *Love and the World: A Guide to Conscious Soul Practice.* Great Barrington, MA: Lindisfarne Books, 2001.

Schafer, William M. *Roaming Free Inside the Cage: a Daoist Approach to the Enneagram.* New York, NY: iUniverse, 2009.

Singer, Michael A. *The Untethered Soul: A Journey Beyond Yourself.* Oakland, CA: Noetic Books, 2007.

Nancy Poitou, "The Tao of Relationships," 1999, The Psyche in Psychology Home, http://mysite.verizon.net/nancy_poiyou/thetaorelate.htm.

"The Heart is More Than We Know." Vol 2 November 2000, Heartmath Institute, www.spiritofmaat.com/archive/nov1/hmath.htm.

Todeschi, Kevin. *Edgar Cayce on Soul Mates: Unlocking the Dynamics of Soul Attraction.* Virginia Beach, VA: A.R.E Press, 1999.

Wolfe, Robert. *Original Wisdom: Stories on an Ancient Way of Knowing.* Rochester, VT: Inner Traditions, 2001.

CPSIA information can be obtained
at www.ICGtesting.com
Printed in the USA
LVOW08s1028161216
517571LV00001B/242/P